Library of
Davidson College

FRIENDS ON THE SHELF

FRIENDS ON THE SHELF

BY

BRADFORD TORREY

"I must get back to my friends on the shelf"
Edward FitzGerald

KENNIKAT PRESS
Port Washington, N. Y./London

809
T694f

71-5914

FRIENDS ON THE SHELF

First published in 1906
Reissued in 1970 by Kennikat Press
Library of Congress Catalog Card No: 70-108709
SBN 8046-0927-6

Manufactured by Taylor Publishing Company   Dallas, Texas

ESSAY AND GENERAL LITERATURE INDEX REPRINT SERIES

CONTENTS

WILLIAM HAZLITT	1
EDWARD FITZGERALD	43
THOREAU	89
THOREAU'S DEMAND UPON NATURE	131
ROBERT LOUIS STEVENSON	151
A RELISH OF KEATS	195
ANATOLE FRANCE	227
VERBAL MAGIC	275
QUOTABILITY	289
THE GRACE OF OBSCURITY	309
IN DEFENSE OF THE TRAVELER'S NOTEBOOK	319
CONCERNING THE LACK OF AN AMERICAN LITERATURE	329

WILLIAM HAZLITT

WILLIAM HAZLITT

HAPPY is the man who enjoys *himself*. His are the true riches. Saving physical pain and mortal illness, few evils can touch him. He may lose friends and make enemies; all the powers of the world may seem to have combined against him; he may work hard and fare worse; poverty may sit at his table and share his bed; but he is not to be greatly pitied. His good things are within. He enjoys him*self*. He has found the secret that the rest of men are all, more or less consciously, looking for, — how to be happy though miserable. It seems an easy method; nothing could be less complicated: simply to enjoy one's own mind. The thing is to do it.

Whether any one ever really accomplished the miracle for more than brief intervals at once, a skeptic may doubt; but some have believed themselves to have accomplished it; and in questions of this intimately personal nature, the difference between faith and fact is small and unimportant. It is of the essence of belief not to be disturbed overmuch by theoretical objections. If I am happy, what is it to me that my busybody of a neighbor across the way has settled it with himself that I am not happy, and in the nature of the case cannot be? Let my meddlesome neighbor mind his own affairs. The pudding is mine, not his; and, with or without his leave, the proof of the pudding is in the eating.

These not very uncommonplace reflections are suggested by the remembrance of what are reported to have been the last words of the man whose name stands at the head of this paper. He was dying before his time, in what the world, if it had happened to concern itself about so inconsiderable an event, would have called rather squalid circumstances. His life had mostly been cloudy. The greater part of his fifty-two years had been spent in quarreling impartially with friends and foes, and, strange to say (matters terrestrial being habitually so out of joint), the logical result had followed. His domestic experiences, too, had been little to his comfort and less to his credit. So far as women were concerned, he had played the fool to his heart's content and his enemies' amusement. Of his two wives (both living), neither was now at his bedside. His purse was empty, or near it. It was almost a question how he should be buried. Withal, as a man more than ordinarily ambitious, he had never done the things he had cared most to do; and now it was all over. And being always an eloquent man, and having breath for one sentence more, he said, "Well, I have had a happy life."

Nor need it be assumed that he was either lying or posing. With abundance of misfortune and no lack of disappointment, with outward things working pretty unanimously against him, he had enjoyed himself. In a word, he remained to the last what he had been from the first, a sentimentalist; and a sentimentalist, like a Christian, has joys that the world knows not of.

For a sentimentalist is one who, more than the majority of his fellows, cultivates and relishes his emotions. They are the chief of his living, the choicest of his crop, his "best of dearest and his only care;"

as why should they not be, since they give him the most of what he most desires? Perhaps we should all be sentimentalists if we could. As it is, the number of such is relatively small, though even at that they may be said to be of various kinds, as their emotions are excited by various classes of objects.

If a man's nature is religious, his sentimentalism, supposing him to have been born with that gift, naturally takes on a religious turn; he treasures the luxury of contrition and the raptures of assured forgiveness. Like one of the earliest and most celebrated of his kind, he can feed day and night upon tears, — having plentiful occasion, perhaps, for such a watery diet, — and be the more ecstatic in proportion as he sounds more and more deeply the unfathomable depths of his unworthiness. This, in part at least, is what is meant by the current phrase, "enjoying religion." Devotional literature bears unbroken witness to its reality and fervors, from the Psalms of David down to the "Lives of the Saints" and the diaries of latter-day Methodism. There is nothing sweeter to the finer sorts of human nature than devotional self-effacement, whether it be sought as Nirvâna in the silence of a Buddhist's cell, or as a gift of special grace in a tumultuous chorus of "Oh, to be nothing, nothing," at a crowded conventicle. Small wonder that the

> "willing soul would stay
> In such a frame as this,
> And sit and sing itself away
> To everlasting bliss."

Small wonder, surely; for, say what you will (and the remark is not half so much a truism as it sounds), one of the surest ways to be happy is to have happy feelings.

This cultivation of the religious sensibilities is probably the commonest, as at its best it is certainly the noblest form of what, meaning no offense, — though the word has been in bad company, and will never recover from the smirch, — we have called sentimentalism. But there are other forms, suited to other grades of human capacity, for all men are not saints.

There is, for example, especially in these modern times, a purely poetic susceptibility to the charms of the natural world;

so that the favored subject of it, not every day, to be sure, but as often as the mood is upon him, shall experience joys ineffable,

"Trances of thought and mountings of the mind,"

at the sight of an ordinary landscape or the meanest of common flowers.

Of a much lower sort is the sentimentalism of such a man as Sterne; a something not poetical, only half real, a kind of rhetorical trick, never so neatly done, but still a trick, and whatever of genuine feeling there is in it so alloyed with baser metal that even while you enjoy to the very marrow the amazing perfection of the writing (for it would be hard to name another book in which there are so many perfect sentences to the page as in the "Sentimental Journey"), — even while you feel all this, you feel also what a relief it would be to speak a piece of your mind to the smirking, winking, face-making clergyman, who has such pretty feelings, and makes such incomparably pretty copy out of them, but who will by no means allow you to forget that he, as well as another, is a man of flesh and blood (especially flesh), knowing a thing or two of the world in spite of his cloth, and able, if he only would (though of course he won't), to play the rake as handsomely as the next man. A strange candidate for holy orders he surely was, even in a country where a parish is frankly recognized as a "living"! It is a comfort to be assured, on the high authority of Mr. Bagehot, that the only respect in which he resembled a clergyman of our own time was, that he lost his voice and traveled abroad to find it.

And once more, not to refine upon the point unduly, there are such men as Rousseau and Hazlitt; not great poets, like Wordsworth, nor mere professional dealers in the pathetic, like Sterne, but men of literary genius very exceptionally endowed with the dangerous gift of sensibility; which gift, wisely or unwisely, they have nourished and made the most of, first for their own exquisite pleasure in it, and afterward, it may well be, for the sake of its very considerable value as a literary "asset."

Rousseau and Hazlitt, we say; for though the two are in some respects greatly unlike, they are plainly of the same school. For better or worse, the English boy came early under the Frenchman's influence, and, to his credit be it spoken, he was never slow to acknowledge the debt thus incurred. His passion for the "New Éloise" was in time outgrown, but the "Confessions" he "never tired of." He loved to run over in memory the dearer parts of them: Rousseau's "first meeting with Madame Warens, the pomp of sound with which he has celebrated her name, beginning 'Louise-Éléonore de Warens était une demoiselle de La Tour de Pil, noble et ancienne famille de Vevai, ville du pays de Vaud' (sounds which we still tremble to repeat); his description of her person, her angelic smile, her mouth of the size of his own; his walking out one day while the bells were chiming to vespers, and anticipating in a sort of waking dream the life he afterward led with her, in which months and years, and life itself, passed away in undisturbed felicity; the sudden disappointment of his hopes; his transport thirty years after at seeing the same flower which they had brought home together from one of their rambles near Chambéry; his thoughts in that long interval of time; his suppers with Grimm and Diderot after he came to Paris; . . . his literary projects, his fame, his misfortunes, his unhappy temper; his last solitary retirement on the lake and island of Bienne, with his dog and his boat; his reveries and delicious musings there — all these crowd into our minds with recollections which we do not choose to express. There are no passages in the 'New Éloise' of equal force and beauty with the best descriptions in the 'Confessions,' if we except the excursion on the water, Julie's last letter to St. Preux, and his letter to her, recalling the days of their first love. We spent two whole years in reading these two works, and (gentle reader, it was when we were young) in shedding tears over them,

> 'as fast as the Arabian trees
> Their medicinal gums.'

They were the happiest years of our life. We may well say of them, sweet is the dew of their memory, and pleasant the balm of their recollection!"

The whole passage is characteristic and illuminating. Hazlitt is speaking of another, but as writers will and must, whether they mean it or not, he is disclosing himself. The boyish reader's tears, the grown man's trembling at the sound of the eloquent French words, and the confession of the concluding sentence (which he repeated word for word years afterward in the essay, "On Reading Old Books") — here we have the real Hazlitt, or rather one of the real Hazlitts.

He was strong in memory. His very darkest times — and they were dark enough — he could brighten with sunny recollections: of a painting, it might be, seen twenty years before, and loved ever since; of a favorite actor in a favorite part; of a book read in his youth ("the greatest pleasure in life is that of reading, while we are young"); of the birds that flitted about his path in happier mornings; of the taste of frost-bitten barberries eaten thirty years before, when he was five years old, on the side of King-Oak Hill, in Weymouth,[1]

---

[1] In this Old Colony town, though none of his English biographers appear to know it, the boy Hazlitt lived in the Old

Massachusetts, and never tasted since; of the tea-gardens at Walworth, to which his father used to take him. Oh yes, he can see those gardens still, though he no longer visits them. He has only to "unlock the casket of memory," and a new sense comes over him, as in a dream; his eyes "dazzle," his sensations are all "glossy, spruce, voluptuous, and fine." What luscious adjectives! And how shamelessly, like an innocent, sweet-toothed child, he rolls them under his tongue! Their goodness is inexpressible. But listen to him for another sentence or two, and see what a favor of Providence it is for a writer of essays to be a lover of his own feelings: "I see the beds of larkspur with purple eyes; tall hollyhocks, red or yellow; the broad sunflowers, caked in gold, with bees buzzing round them; wildernesses of pinks, and hot, glowing peonies; poppies run to seed;

North Parsonage, in which had lived some time before a girl named Abigail Smith, afterward better known as Abigail Adams, wife of the second President of the United States, and mother of the sixth. For which fact, more interesting to him than to his readers, it is to be feared, the present writer is indebted to the researches of his old Weymouth schoolmate, now President of the Weymouth Historical Society, Mr. John J. Loud.

the sugared lily, and faint mignonette, all ranged in order, and as thick as they can grow; the box-tree borders; the gravel walks, the painted alcove, the confectionery, the clotted cream: — I think I see them now with sparkling looks; or have they vanished while I have been writing this description of them? No matter; they will return again when I least think of them. All that I have observed since of flowers and plants and grass-plots seem to me borrowed from 'that first garden of my innocence' — to be slips and scions stolen from that bed of memory."

How eloquent he grows! "Slips and scions stolen from that bed of memory!" The very words, simple as they are, and homely as is their theme, throb with emotion, and move as if to music. "Most eloquent of English essayists," his latest biographer pronounces him; and, whether we agree with the judgment or not (sweeping assertions cost little, and contribute to readability), at least we recognize the quality that the biographer has in mind.

A sentimentalist, of all men, knows how to live his good days over again. Pleasure, to his thrifty way of thinking, is not a thing to be enjoyed once, and so done with. He will eat his cake and have it too. Nor shall it be the mere shadow of a feast. Nay, if there is to be any difference to speak of, the second serving shall be better and more substantial than the first. To him nothing else is quite so real as the past. He rejoices in it as in an unchangeable, indefeasible possession. "The past at least is secure." If the present hour is dark and lonely and friendless, he has only to run back and walk again in sunny, flower-bespangled fields, hand in hand with his own boyhood.

Such was Hazlitt's practice as a sentimental economist, and it would take an unusually bold Philistine, we think, to maintain that it was altogether a bad one. The words that he wrote of Rousseau are applicable to himself: "He seems to gather up the past moments of his being like drops of honey-dew to distil a precious liquor from them." To vary a phrase of Mr. Pater's, he is a master in the art of impassioned recollection.

It makes little difference where he is, or

what circumstance sets him going. He may be among the Alps. "Clarens is on my left," he says, "the Dent de Jamant is behind me, the rocks of Meillerie opposite: under my feet is a green bank, enamelled with white and purple flowers, in which a dewdrop here and there glitters with pearly light. Intent upon the scene and upon the thoughts that stir within me, I conjure up the cheerful passages of my life, and a crowd of happy images appear before me." Or he is in London, and hears the tinkle of the "Letter-Bell" as it passes. "It strikes upon the ear, it vibrates to the brain, it wakes me from the dream of time, it flings me back upon my first entrance into life, the period of my first coming up to town, when all around was strange, uncertain, adverse, — a hubbub of confused noises, a chaos of shifting objects, — and when this sound alone, startling me with the recollection of a letter I had to send to the friends I had lately left, brought me as it were to myself, made me feel that I had links still connecting me with the universe, and gave me hope and patience to persevere. At that loud-tinkling, interrupted sound, the long line of blue hills near the place where I was brought up waves in the horizon, a golden sunset hovers over them, the dwarf oaks rustle their red leaves in the evening breeze, and the road from Wem to Shrewsbury, by which I first set out on my journey through life, stares me in the face as plain, but, from time and change, as visionary and mysterious, as the pictures in the 'Pilgrim's Progress.'"

"When a man has arrived at a certain ripeness in intellect," says Keats, "any one grand and spiritual passage serves him as a starting-post towards all 'the two-and-thirty Palaces.'" Yes, and some men will go a good way on the same royal road, with no more spiritual incitement than the passing of the postman.

How fondly Hazlitt recalls the day of days when he met Coleridge, and walked with him six miles homeward; when "the very milestones had ears, and Hamer Hill stooped with all its pines, to listen to a poet as he passed." At the sixth milepost man and boy separated. "On my way back," says Hazlitt, "I had a sound in my ears —

it was the voice of Fancy; I had a light before me — it was the face of Poetry." A second meeting had been agreed upon, and meanwhile the boy's soul was possessed by "an uneasy, pleasurable sensation," thinking of what was in store for him. "During those months the chill breath of winter gave me a welcoming; the vernal air was balm and inspiration to me. The golden sunsets, the silver star of evening, lighted me on my way to new hopes and prospects. *I was to visit Coleridge in the spring.*"

Verily, the words of the dying man begin to sound less paradoxical. He *had* been happy. If his buffetings and disappointments had been more than fall to the lot of average humanity, so had been his joys and his triumphs. He had more *capacity* for joy. Therein, in great part, lay his genius. To borrow a good word from Jeremy Taylor, all his perceptions were "quick and full of relish." Even his sorrows, once they were far enough behind him, became only a purer and more ethereal kind of bliss. So he tells us, in one of his later essays, how he loved best of all to lie whole mornings on a sunny bank on Salisbury Plain, with no object before him, neither knowing nor caring how the time passed, his thoughts floating like motes before his half-shut eyes, or some image of the past rushing by him — "Diana and her fawn, and all the glories of the antique world." "Then," he adds, "I start away to prevent the iron from entering my soul, and let fall some tears into that stream of time which separates me farther and farther from all I once loved." Whether the tears were physical or metaphorical, whether they wet the cheek or only the printed page, the man who shed them is not, on their account, to be regarded as an object of commiseration. Sadness that can be thus described, in words so like the fabled nightingale's song, "most musical, most melancholy," is more to be desired than much that goes by the name of pleasure, and the deeper and more poignant the emotion, the more precious are its returns.

Nobody ever understood this better than Hazlitt. His sentimentalism, as we call it, was no ignorant, superficial gift of young-ladyish sensibility. It had intellectual foundations. He felt because he knew. He had been intimate with himself; he had cherished his own consciousness. He remarks somewhere that the three perfect egotists of the race were Rousseau, Wordsworth, and Benvenuto Cellini. He would defy the world, he said, to name a fourth. But he might easily enough have named the fourth himself, had not modesty — or something else — prevented. If he had lived longer, he would perhaps have written the fourth man's autobiography; his formal autobiography, that is to say. In fact, though not in name, he had already written it; some might be ready to maintain (but they would be wrong) that he had written little else. By "egotism" he meant not selfishness in the more ordinary, mercantile acceptation of the word, — a lack of benevolence, an extravagant desire to be better off than others in the way of worldly "goods," — but the very quality we have been trying to show forth: absorption in one's own mind, a profound and perpetual consciousness of one's own being, the habit of interfusing self and outward things till distinctions of spirit and matter, finite and infinite, self and the universe, are for the moment almost done away with, and feeling is all in all.

This, or something like this, was Hazlitt's secret. This is the breath of life that throbs in the best of his pages. Whatever subject he handled, a prize-fight, a game of fives, a juggler's trick, a play of Shakespeare, a picture of Titian, the pleasure of painting, he did it not simply *con amore*, or, as his newer critics say, with gusto (the word is Hazlitt's own — he wrote an essay about it), but as if the thing were for the time being part and parcel of himself. And so, oftener than is commonly to be expected of essay-writers, his sentences are not so much vivid as alive.

More than most men, he was alive himself. In Keats's phrase, he felt existence. There was no telling its preciousness to him. The essay "On the Feeling of Immortality in Youth," though at the end it breaks out despairingly into something like the old cry, *Vanitas vanitatum*, is filled to the brim with a passionate love of this present world. The idea of leaving it is abhorrent to him. To think what he has been, and what he has enjoyed, in those good days of his; days when he "looked for hours at a Rembrandt without being conscious of the flight of time;" days of the "full, pulpy feeling of youth, tasting existence and every object in it." What a bliss to be young! Then life is new, and, for all we know of it, endless. As for old age and death, they are no concern of ours. "Like a rustic at a fair, we are full of amazement and rapture, and have no thought of going home, or that it will soon be night." Sentences like this must have been what Keats had in mind when he spoke so lovingly of "distilled prose;" prose that bears repetition and brooding over, like exquisite verse. Some sentences, indeed, are better than whole books, and this of Hazlitt's is one of them; as fine, almost, — as purely "distilled," — as that famous kindred one of Sir William Temple: "When all is done, human life is, at the greatest and the best, but like a froward child, that must be played with and humored a little to keep it quiet till it falls asleep, and then the care is over."

And since we are quoting (and few authors invite quotation more than Hazlitt, as few have themselves quoted more constantly), let us please ourselves with another sentence from the same essay, — a page-long roll-call of a sentimental man's beatitudes, turning at the close to a sudden blackness of darkness: —

"To see the golden sun, the azure sky, the outstretched ocean; to walk upon the green earth, and be lord of a thousand creatures; to look down yawning precipices or over distant sunny vales; to see the world spread out under one's feet on a map; to bring the stars near; to view the smallest insects through a microscope; to read history, and consider the revolutions of empire and the successions of generations; to hear of the glory of Tyre, of Sidon, of Babylon, and of Susa, and to say all these were before me and are now nothing; to say I exist in such a point of time and in such a point of space; to be a spectator and a part of its ever-moving scene; to witness the change of season, of spring and autumn, of winter and summer; to feel heat and cold, pleasure and pain, beauty and deformity, right and wrong; to be sensible to the accidents of nature; to consider the mighty world of eye and ear; to listen to the stock-dove's notes amid the forest deep; to journey over moor and mountain; to hear the midnight sainted choir; to visit lighted halls, or the cathedral's gloom, or sit in crowded theatres and see life itself mocked; to study the works of art and refine the sense of beauty to agony; to worship fame, and to dream of immortality; to look upon the Vatican, and to read Shakespeare; to gather up the wisdom of the ancients, and to pry into the future; to listen to the trump of war, the shout of victory; to question history as to the movements of the human heart; to seek for truth; to plead the cause of humanity; to overlook the world as if time and nature poured their treasures at our feet — to be and to do all this, and then in a moment to be nothing!"

"To look upon the Vatican, and to read Shakespeare!" Once more we are reminded of Keats, a man very different from Hazlitt in many ways, but, like him, "a near neighbor to himself," and

WILLIAM HAZLITT

a worshiper of beauty. "Things real," says Keats, "such as existences of sun, moon and stars — and passages of Shakespeare."

Hazlitt's nature was peculiarly intense, with the very slightest admixture of those saner and commoner elements that keep our poor humanity, in its ordinary manifestations, comparatively reasonable and sweet. His years, from what we read of them, seem to have passed in one long state of feverishness. He cannot have been a pleasant man either for himself or for any one else to live with. Self-absorbed, irascible, and proud, with little or no gift of humor (sentimentalists as a class seem to be deficient in this quality, the case of Sterne to the contrary notwithstanding; and Sterne's humor is perhaps only an additional reason for suspecting that his fine sentiments were mostly literary), he had a splendid capacity for hating, and was possessed of a kind of ugly courage that made it easy for him to speak with extraordinary plainness of other men's defects. If the men happened to be his friends, so much the better. He professed, indeed, to like a friend all the more for having "faults that one could talk about." "Put a pen in his hand," says Mr. Birrell, "and he would say anything." Whatever he said or did, suffered or enjoyed, it was all with a kind of passion. As the common saying is, there was no halfway work with him. It could never be complained of him, as he complained of some other writer, that his sentences wanted impetus. He understood the value of surprise, and never balked at an extreme statement. Thus he would say, in the coolest manner imaginable, "It is utterly impossible to persuade an editor that he is nobody." As if it really were! As if it were not ten times nearer impossible to persuade a contributor that *he* is nobody!

On his way to the famous prize-fight, — famous because he was there, — spending the night at an inn crowded with the "Fancy," he overheard a "tall English yeoman" holding forth to those about him concerning "rent, and taxes, and the price of corn." One of his hearers ventured at a certain point to interpose an objection, whereupon the yeoman bore down upon

WILLIAM HAZLITT

him with the word, "Confound it, man, don't be insipid." "Thinks I to myself," says Hazlitt, "that's a good phrase." And so it was, and quite in his own line. "There is no surfeiting on gall," he remarks somewhere, with admirable truth. He wrote an essay upon " Cant and Hypocrisy," another upon " Disagreeable People," and another upon the " Pleasure of Hating." And he knew whereof he spake. Sentimentalism — the Hazlitt brand of it, at any rate — is nothing like sweetened water. "If any one wishes to see me quite calm," he says, in his emphatic manner, "they may cheat me in a bargain, or tread upon my toes; but a truth repelled, a sophism repeated, totally disconcerts me, and I lose all patience. I am not, in the ordinary acceptation of the term, a good-natured man." "Lamb," he once remarked, "yearns after and covets what soothes the frailty of human nature." So did not Hazlitt. Lamb delighted in people as such. Even their foibles — especially their foibles, it would be truer to say — were pleasant to him. In short, he was a humorist. Hazlitt's first interest, on the other hand, seems to have been in places and things, — including books and pictures, — and his own thoughts about them. Of human beings he liked personages, so called, men who have done something, — actors, painters, authors, statesmen, and the like. As for the common run of his foolish fellow mortals, if their frailties were to be stroked, by all means let it be done the wrong way. The operation might be less acceptable to the patient, but it would probably do him more good, and would certainly be more amusing to the operator and the lookers-on.

No doubt the man experienced now and then a reaction from his prevailing condition of feverishness. He must have had moods, we may guess, when he saw the beauty and comfort of a quieter way of life. Indeed, he has left one inimitable portrait of a character the exact reverse of his own, a portrait drawn not bitterly nor grudgingly, but in something not altogether unlike the affectionately quizzical spirit of Lamb himself. He calls it the character of a bookworm.

"The person I mean," he says, "has an admiration for learning, if he is only dazzled by its light. He lives among old authors, if he does not enter much into their spirit. He handles the covers, and turns over the page, and is familiar with the names and dates. He is busy and self-involved. He hangs like a film and cobweb upon letters, or is like the dust upon the outside of knowledge, which should not be rudely brushed aside. He follows learning as its shadow; but as such, he is respectable. He browses on the husk and leaves of books, as the young fawn browses on the bark and leaves of trees. Such a one lives all his life in a dream of learning, and has never once had his sleep broken by a real sense of things. He believes implicitly in genius, truth, virtue, liberty, because he finds the names of these things in books. He thinks that love and friendship are the finest things imaginable, both in practice and theory. The legend of good women is to him no fiction.[1] When he steals from the twilight of his cell, the scene breaks upon him like an illuminated missal, and all the people he sees are but so many figures in a *camera obscura*. He

[1] As it was to Solomon and, by this time, to William Hazlitt.

reads the world, like a favorite volume, only to find beauties in it, or like an edition of some old work which he is preparing for the press, only to make emendations in it, and correct the errors that have inadvertently slipt in. He and his dog Tray are much the same honest, simple-hearted, faithful, affectionate creatures — if Tray could but read! His mind cannot take the impression of vice; but the gentleness of his nature turns gall to milk. He would not hurt a fly. He draws the picture of mankind from the guileless simplicity of his own heart; and when he dies, his spirit will take its smiling leave, without ever having had an ill thought of others, or the consciousness of one in itself!"

It would have been for Hazlitt's happiness, or at least for his comfort, if he had possessed a grain or two of his bookworm's "guileless simplicity." But things must be as they must. His name was not Nathanael. He was "dowered with the hate of hate, the scorn of scorn," and it was not in his nature to be patient and easy-going, especially where anything so vitally essential as a difference of opinion touching the character of Napoleon Bonaparte was concerned. He had the qualities of his defects. If he was sometimes too peppery, he was never insipid.

Men write best of matters in which they are most interested and most at home, and of Hazlitt we may say, speaking a little cynically, after his own manner, that with all his multiplicity of topics, he wrote best about his own feelings and his neighbors' infirmities, though as for the latter sort of material, tò be sure, he did not confine himself very strictly to that with which his fellow men furnished him. Proud as he was, indeed (and here we may note another characteristic of the sentimentalist), he had sometimes a really shocking lack of decent personal reserve. During his infatuation with Miss Sarah Walker, as all the world — or all the Hazlitt world — knows, he could not keep his tongue in his head. He would even buttonhole a stranger on a street corner, and unbosom his woes to him at full length in most unmanly fashion: how he loved the girl, and how the girl would not love him, and so on, and so on. And having perpetrated this almost incredible absurdity, he would tell of it afterward; and then, to make matters still worse, when he had recovered from his distemper (always a rapid process in his case), he wrote a book about it. This book is reprinted, all in fair type, in the latest and handsomest edition of his works; but, thank Heaven, we are none of us bound to read it. Nor need we take the whole miserable business too seriously, as if (except on its literary side) it were anything so very far out of the common. It was ridiculous, of course; but so are the love affairs of elderly men generally. Their folly has passed into a proverb. As wise old Izaak Walton — who had two excellent wives of his own, both "of distinguished clerical connexion" — long ago expressed it, "love is a flattering mischief," "a passion that carries us to commit errors with as much ease as whirlwinds move feathers." The good man's assonance would have driven Flaubert insane, but his doctrine is consolatory. A feather may surely be excused for slipping its cable before a whirlwind.

It was only a year or two after the

WILLIAM HAZLITT

conclusion of this distressing episode that Hazlitt, being in Italy, wrote one of the most delightful of his essays, the one upon a sun-dial.

"*Horas non numero nisi serenas* is the motto of a sun-dial near Venice," —so he begins. Then, after descanting upon the exceeding beauty and appropriateness of the Latin words, he falls foul of the French people for the "less *sombre* and less edifying" turn that they are accustomed to give to similar matters. He has seen a clock in Paris bearing a figure of Time seated in a boat, which Cupid is rowing along, with the motto, *L'Amour fait passer le Temps;* a motto that the French wits, it appears, have travestied into *Le Temps fait passer L'Amour*. This is ingenious, he concedes (how could he help it?), but it lacks sentiment. "I like people," he declares, "who have something that they love, and something that they hate." The French "never arrive at the classical—or the romantic." The criticism may or may not be just (it seems a hard saying), but what the average reader of the paragraph is likely to be thinking of, if he happens to be familiar with the story of Hazlitt's own adventures with Cupid, is not any weakness of the French people, but the amusing cleverness with which the Parisian wits have hit off the weakness of a certain literary Englishman. Truly *Le Temps fait passer L'Amour*, — sometimes with deplorable celerity, — on both sides of the Channel.

Naturally, however, nothing of this sort occurred to Hazlitt. His good memory was like the sun-dial, — it counted none but the bright hours. By this time he had almost forgotten both his unhappy passion and the unhappier book that he wrote about it.

And, indeed, it is time that *we* forgot them. For one who has found his profit in strolling up and down in Hazlitt's essays at odd hours for half a lifetime, it is little becoming to talk overmuch about the man's personal imperfections. It matters little to any of us now that his temper was bad; that his passions too often betrayed him into folly; that his faculties lacked a certain balance; that his *mal de rêverie*, whether born with him or caught from his French master, sometimes ran too feverish a course; that, in short, he had the not unusual weaknesses of super-sensitive men. What does matter is that at his best he wrote English prose as comparatively few have written it, and in doing so said a world of bright and memorable things that no one else could have said so well, even if it had ever occurred to any one else to say them at all. If he was difficult to live with, that is a question more than seventy years out of date; and no competent reader ever brought a similar accusation against his essays. It has been said of them more than once, to be sure, that they are not so good as Lamb's; but then, you may say that of all essays; and really the comparison is futile, not to call it foolish. The men were nothing alike; though even so, we may gladly agree with Mr. Henley's comment, that, as "dissimilars," they "go gallantly and naturally together — *par nobile fratrum.*"

Perhaps Hazlitt sometimes wrote too much in haste, with hardly sufficient care for those minute excellences that go to the making of perfection, though he could talk edifyingly under that head, and appears to have been the author of the clever parody, more clever than true, — as cleverness is apt to be, —

> "Learn to write slow: all other graces
> Will follow in their proper places;"

and it may be, as one of the cleverest of his admirers assures us, that he was "really too witty." Concerning points so nice as these, it is hard for "honest and painful men" to feel certain. Haste has the compensatory virtue of generating heat, while as for the having too much wit, it is like having too much money, or more than one's share of personal beauty; serious misfortunes, both of them, beyond a doubt (every one says so), but misfortunes to be put up with, at a pinch, in a spirit of Christian resignation. All things considered, too much is perhaps better than too little, and, for better or worse, excess on both sides of the line is rather Hazlitt's "note." Of the virtues of courage and obstinacy he possessed enough for two. We applaud, even while we pity, to see how, all his life long, he stood up for what he believed to be the truth, in spite of the frowns, and worse than frowns, of all who in that day had it in their power to blast the career of men in his profession. He was defamed and abused, for political reasons, — all for that unlucky Bonapartean bee in his bonnet, — as few men of letters have ever been, and to the last he did not haul down his flag. Let so much be said in his honor. And whatever else is forgotten, let the words of Charles Lamb be remembered: "I should belie my own conscience if I said less than that I think W. H. to be in his natural and healthy state one of the wisest and finest spirits breathing." The most virtuous of those who blame him may count themselves happy ever to receive half so handsome a tribute from so authoritative a source. Human nature is a tangled skein; moral perfection is not to be encountered every day, even among critics. To do one's main stint well is probably as much as most of us can reasonably hope for; and so much, assuredly, Hazlitt did; for his main work, as we see it, was the writing of his few volumes of critical and miscellaneous essays. Into these he put the breath of long life. These are what count, seventy years after. Whoever begins with them, recurs to them. Not one of them but comes under Lamb's heading of "take-downable."

As a matter of course, however, being a man of active mind and having his living to make by his pen, he wrote many things besides these. He began, indeed, with a metaphysical treatise, — a child of his youth (he believed it a great discovery) for which he never ceased to cherish an excusable fondness. This, on the authority of those who have read it, or have talked with some who have done so, we take to be a rather difficult and innutritious choke-pear, something to be safely left alone by ordinary seekers after knowledge. Then, toward the end of his career, he produced a four-volume life of Napoleon, which, on equally good authority, we should think to have been a kind of anticipation or foreshadowing of the modern "novel with a purpose." His latest editors go so far as to leave it out of their fine twelve-volume edition of his works. Somewhere between these two attempts at immortality he indulged himself in a book on grammar, intended especially to correct the errors of Lindley Murray, more particularly, we believe, his faulty definition of a noun as the name of an object. Fortunately or otherwise, this work (every author of consequence has at least one such) never got beyond the original (manuscript) edition. The making of it seems a queer freak for a man of Hazlitt's turn of mind; but then, as Mr. Birrell observes, "grammar has its fascinations; and even such men as John Milton and John Wesley, no less than William Cobbett and William Hazlitt, succumbed to its charm." And he might have added a name more illustrious still,—the name of Julius Cæsar.

All these longer works (including a "Reply to Malthus") we consider ourselves, as readers, at full liberty to skip. Furthermore, we consider their merits or demerits to have no bearing whatever upon the question of their author's standing as an essayist. Like every man who practices an art, he is entitled to be judged, not by his experiments and failures, but by his successes. Wordsworth might have written a thousand "Ecclesiastical Sonnets," instead of only one hundred and thirty odd, and every one of them might have been less imaginative than the one before it, without making him any the less a true and noble poet. For a poet, like the Pope, is infallible only when he is inspired; at other times he may nod as well as another man. Moreover, in the case of the poet, at least, the man himself may not be sure whether or not, at any given moment, the divine afflatus is upon him. It was Doctor Johnson, a poet himself, and the biographer of poets, who said that it was easy enough to make verses; he had made a hundred in a day; the difficulty was to know when you had made a good one. And the same difficulty, in a less degree, is encountered by the maker of prose essays. It is a wise father that knows his own child. Nor in such a matter have a man's contemporaries any great advantage over the man himself. The folly of their judgments is proverbial. It is necessary to wait. Apparently there is some strange virtue in the mere lapse of time. "Time will tell," the common people say; and the scholar has no better wisdom. Hazlitt must stand his trial with the rest. Sooner or later the years will render their verdict, though none of us may live long enough to hear it. The best that can be said now is, that so far the balloting seems to be strongly in his favor.

EDWARD FITZGERALD

EDWARD FITZGERALD

"I HAVE been reading a good deal, but not much in the way of knowledge." So the future translator of Omar Khayyám wrote to a friend in 1832, being then twenty-three years old, and two years out of the University. The words may be taken as fairly descriptive of the remaining fifty years of his life. He was always reading something, but not with an eye to rank or scholarship. His old friends and schoolfellows one after another stepped into high place. Tennyson, Thackeray, and Carlyle were names on every tongue; Spedding, less talked about, was deep in a *magnum opus;* Thompson, Donne, Peacock, Allen, and Cowell held positions of honor in church or college; but FitzGerald had buried himself of set purpose in an insignificant, out-of-the-way Suffolk village, and, by his own account of himself, was dozing away his years in "visionary inactivity,"—in "the enjoyment of old childish habits and sympathies."

Not less truly than his mates, however, as it now appears, he was living his own life; and perhaps not less truly than the foremost of them he was to come into lasting renown. Such are the "diversities of operations," through which the spirit of man develops and discloses itself.

FitzGerald came of an eccentric family. "We are all mad," he wrote; and his own share of the ancestral inheritance—mostly of an amiable and amusing sort—early made itself evident. While he was at Cambridge, his mother drove up to the college gate in her coach and four, and sent for him to come down and see her; but he could not go,—his only pair of shoes was at the cobbler's. The Suffolk friend, from whom we have this anecdote, adds that to the last FitzGerald was perfectly careless of dress. "I can see him now," he says, "walking down into Woodbridge, with an old Inverness cape, a double-breasted flowered satin waistcoat, slippers on his feet, and a handkerchief, very likely, tied over his hat." It was odd, no doubt, that a gentleman should dress in so unconventional a manner; but it was much odder that he should write to Mrs. Kemble a fortnight after the death of his brother, in 1879: "I say but little of my brother's death. We were very good friends, of very different ways of thinking; I had not been within side his lawn gates (three miles off) these dozen years (no fault of his), and I did not enter them at his funeral — which you will very likely — and properly — think wrong." Only an eccentric man could have had occasion to say that; and surely none but a very eccentric man *would* have said it.

After leaving the University, — at which, by the way, he barely obtained his degree, — he went to Paris (where he had spent part of his boyhood), but stayed only a month or two; and on his return, having just passed his majority, he wrote to Allen, "Tell Thackeray that he is never to invite me to his house, as I intend never to go." He would rather go there than anywhere else, to be sure; but he has got "all sorts of Utopian ideas" about society into his head, and is "going to become a great bear."

In another man's mouth this might have been merely the expression of a passing whim; but whether FitzGerald meant the words seriously or not, they were pretty accurately fulfilled. His friends were of the noblest and truest, and his affection for them was of the warmest and stanchest, no man's more so; but he chose to live apart.

"Why, sir," said Doctor Johnson to Boswell, "you find no man, at all intellectual, who is willing to leave London. No, sir, when a man is tired of London, he is tired of life; for there is in London all that life can afford." And Boswell, of course, responded Amen. "I can talk twice as much in London as anywhere else," he remarked, with Boswellian simplicity. Possibly FitzGerald was less "intellectual" than the great luminary and his satellite; or perhaps his intellectuality, such as it was, ran less exclusively to talk.[1] At all events, he hated London as a place of residence; and even when he paid it a

[1] "Mr. Johnson, indeed, as he was a very talking man himself, had an idea that nothing promoted happiness so much as conversation." — Mrs. Piozzi.

visit, he was always in such feverish and ludicrous haste to get away that he was sure to leave his calls and errands no more than half done. "I long to spread wing and fly into the kind clear air of the country," he writes on one occasion of this sort. "I see nobody in the streets half so handsome as Mr. Reynolds of our parish. . . . A great city is a deadly plague. . . . I get radishes to eat for breakfast of a morning; with them comes a savor of earth that brings all the delicious gardens of the world back into one's soul, and almost draws tears from one's eyes." In the mouth of a man of social position, University training, and independent fortune, — who had lived in Paris, and was only thirty-five years old, — language like this bespeaks a born rustic and recluse, not to say a philosopher. And such FitzGerald was.

Not that he craved a life in the wilderness (being neither a John the Baptist nor a René), or had any extraordinary appreciation of the beauties of nature, so called. There was little of Wordsworth or of Thoreau in his composition, or, if there was, it seldom found expression; but he detested crowds, was ill at ease in society, and having a bent toward homely solitude, was independent enough to follow it. It must seem queer to his old friends, he knew, but he preferred to "poke about in the country," using his books, as ladies do their knitting work, to pass the time away. Here is one of his days, a day of "glorious sunshine:" —

"All the morning I read about Nero in Tacitus, lying at full length on a bench in the garden: a nightingale singing, and some red anemones eyeing the sun manfully not far off. A funny mixture all this: Nero, and the delicacy of spring; all very human, however. Then at half past one lunch on Cambridge cream cheese; then a ride over hill and dale: then spudding up some weeds from the grass: and then coming in, I sit down to write to you, my sister winding red worsted from the back of a chair, and the most delightful little girl in the world chattering incessantly. So runs the world away. You think I live in epicurean ease: but this happens to be a jolly day: one is n't always well, or tolerably good, the weather is not always clear, nor nightingales singing, nor Tacitus full of pleasant atrocity. But such as life is, I believe I have got hold of a good end of it."

Sometimes, it must be owned, he seemed not quite to approve of his own choice. "Men ought to have an ambition to stir and travel, and fill their heads and senses." So he says once, in an unusual mood of something like penitence. Even then, however, he concludes, characteristically, "but so it is." There speaks the real FitzGerald. He is what he is, what he was made: a man without ambition; a man incapable, from first to last, of taking himself seriously. He could never have said, as Tennyson did in his youth, and in effect for all his life, "I mean to be famous." If FitzGerald meant to be anything, — which is doubtful, — he meant to be obscure. The wonder of it all is that his life was beautiful, his spirit sweet, and his posthumous reward celebrity.

He had little or none of the melancholy which so generally accompanies the union of exceptional powers with an enfeebled will and a comparative intellectual sterility. For one thing, he seems to have been spared the persecution of friends. As he expected little of himself, so they expected little of him. Unlike most men of a kindred sort — men of whom Gray and Amiel may stand as typical examples — he was left to go his own gait. Nobody wrote to him week after week, chiding him for his indolence and entreating him to produce a masterpiece. Happy man that he was, his youth had held out no promise of such production, and so his subsequent course was not clouded by the shadow of a promise unfulfilled. If he was down in the country letting the moss grow over him, why, it was only "old Fitz," from whom nobody had ever looked for anything very different. So Thackeray, Tennyson, and the rest seem to have thought. And so thought the man himself. Life was worth living; oh yes; and he had "got hold of a good end of it;" but it was hardly a thing to disquiet one's self about. He set little value upon time or money, and correspondingly little upon his own gifts. There were always hours enough, and more than enough, for the nothings he had to do; his income was sufficient; if it declined, — as it did, — it was no matter, he had only to reduce his expenditures; he never earned a penny, or considered the possibility of doing so; and withal, he was not made to write anything himself, but to please himself with the writings of others.

He was born of the school of Epicurus. His aim was to pass the time quietly; pitching his desires low, never overmuch in earnest, taking things as they came, —

"Crowning the present, doubting of the rest;"

"not a hero, not even a philosopher, but a quiet, humane, and prudent man;" cultivating no enthusiasm, and aiming at no perfection. For fifty years he seems to have been a consistent vegetarian. Like the master of his school, — whom he seldom or never mentions, and of whom he perhaps as seldom thought, — he subsisted mostly on bread, and drank wine sparingly. Such a diet gave him lightness of spirits, he said, — a better thing, surely, than any tickling of the palate.

With his liking for the country — in

which, again, he was at one with his unrecognized master — went a strong and persistent preference for the society of common people. For correspondents he had always scholars and men of note, the best of his time, and many of them; for daily associates he chose a sailor, a village clergyman's family, and an old woman or two. One of the greatest men he had ever known was his sailor, the captain of his yacht, — "my captain," he calls him; "a gentleman of nature's grandest type," "fit to be king of a kingdom as well as of a lugger." From Lowestoft he sends word to Laurence, the portrait painter, "I came here a few days ago, for the benefit of my old doctor, the sea, and my captain's company, which is as good." One who knew him at the time of his intimacy with Bernard Barton, the Quaker poet (fortunate Quaker, with Lamb and Fitz-Gerald both writing letters to him!), describes him as living in a little cottage at Boulge, a mile from the village, on the edge of his father's park, with no companion save a parrot and a Skye terrier. Such domestic duties as he did not attend to with his own hands were performed by an "old-fashioned Suffolk woman." It was at this period that FitzGerald — then thirty-three years old — wrote to Barton, "I believe I should like to live in a small house just outside a pleasant English town all the days of my life, making myself useful in a humble way, reading my books, and playing a rubber of whist at night." And it may be added that few men have ever come nearer to realizing their own dream.

The Hall was mostly unoccupied in those days, though "the great lady" — FitzGerald's mother — would be there once in a while, and "would drive about in a coach of four black horses." So says the son of the village rector, who adds that FitzGerald "used to walk by himself, slowly, with a Skye terrier." The rector's son (a grandson, by the bye, of the poet Crabbe) was rather afraid of his "grave, middle-aged" neighbor. "He seemed a proud and very punctilious man . . . never very happy or light-hearted, though his conversation was most amusing sometimes." On this last point we have also the testimony of his housekeeper, the "old-fashioned Suffolk woman" before mentioned. "So kind he was," she says; "not never one to make no obstacles. Such a joking gentleman he was, too!" All his dependents, indeed, speak of his kindness. A boy of the village, who was employed to read to him in the evening during his later years, told Mr. Groome [1] "how Mr. FitzGerald always gave him plenty of plum cake, and how they used to play piquet together. Only sometimes a tame mouse would come out and sit on the table, and then not a card must be dropped." "A pretty picture," Mr. Groome calls it. And so say we.

As to the picture of FitzGerald's manner of life taken as a whole, it will be thought "pretty" or not according to the prepossessions of the reader. To many it will seem in all respects amiable, a refreshment to read about. Why should a man not be what he was made to be? If he likes the heat of battle, let him fight, so that he does it fairly and with those who enjoy the same game. If another man cares not to

[1] Author of *Two Suffolk Friends*.

be strenuous, but only to pass his day innocently, with pleasure to himself and harm to nobody else, — why, the world is big enough; let him be at liberty to sit in his corner and see the crowd go by.

"'An hour we have,' thou saidst. 'Ah, waste it well.'"

And after all, the idler may reach the goal as soon as some who hurry. The race ought to be his who has trained hardest and run hardest; and it would be, perhaps, if the world were logically and properly governed; but things being as they are, the experience of mankind seems to show a measure of truth in the old Hebrew paradox, "The race is not to the swift." Whether it is or not, the question had no particular interest for FitzGerald. His thoughts were not of winning a prize. His temperament had put him out of the competition. Temperament is fatality; and he was content to have it so. "It is not my talent," he said, "to take the tide at its flow." In his "predestined Plot of Dust and Soul" the vine of worldly prudence had never struck root.

He was peculiar in other ways. He was

constitutionally a skeptic. Many things which he had been taught to believe seemed to him insufficiently established; improbable, if not incredible. The Master of Trinity wrote of him and of one of his dearest friends, "Two of the purest-living men among my intimates, FitzGerald and Spedding, were prisoners in Doubting Castle all their lives, or at least the last half of them." The language is euphemistic. Some calamities are so deeply felt that it is natural to veil allusion to them under metaphor. His friends, the Master means to say, had lost their faith in the tenets of the English Church. "A great problem," he pronounces it. And such it surely was: that two such men — "pure-living men!" — should doubt of matters which to so many bishops, priests, and deacons are the very certainties of existence. But so it is. Some men seem to be born for unbelief; and out of that number a few are so nonconformative, so perverse, or so honest as to live according to their lights. Concerning questions of this kind FitzGerald said little either in public or private. An unheroic, peace-loving man, who wishes to slip through the world unnoticed, naturally keeps some thoughts to himself, growing them, to borrow Keats's phrase, in "a philosophic back-garden." He reasoned about them, it would seem, in a quiet spirit, patient, perhaps half indifferent, being happily free from any corroding curiosity as to the origin and destiny of things. In that regard Nature had been good to him. What could not be known, he could get on without knowing. Why wear out one's teeth in champing an iron bit? He spoke his mind, anonymously, in his translation of the Omar Khayyám quatrains, — which are perhaps rather more skeptical than the book of Ecclesiastes, — and once, at least, he shut the lips of a man whom he thought a meddler. The rector of Woodbridge, we are told by Mr. Groome, called on FitzGerald to express his regret at never seeing him at church. We may surmise that the "regret" was expressed in a rather lofty and dogmatic tone, a tone not unnatural, surely, in the case of one clothed with supernatural authority. "Sir," said FitzGerald, whose fondness for clergymen's society was one of his marked characteristics, "you might have conceived that a man has not come to my years without thinking much of these things. I believe I may say that I have reflected on them fully as much as yourself. You need not repeat this visit."

His correspondence, by which mainly the world knows him, is full of interesting revelations. His whims and foibles, and his own gentle amusement over them; his bookish likes and dislikes, one as hearty as the other; his affection for his friends, whose weak points he could sometimes lay a pretty sharp finger on, notwithstanding, frankness being almost always one of an odd man's virtues; his delight in the sea and in his garden ("Don't you love the oleander? I rather worship mine," he writes to Mrs. Kemble); his pottering over translations from the Spanish, the Persian, and the Greek ("all very well; only very little affairs:" he feels "ashamed" when his friend Thompson inquires about them); his music, wherein his taste was simple but difficult (he played without technique and sang without a voice, loving to "recollect some of 'Fidelio' on the pianoforte," and counting it more enjoyable "to perform in one's head one of Handel's choruses" than to hear most Exeter Hall performances), — all these things, and many more, come out in his letters, which are never anything *but* letters, written to please his friends, — and himself, — with no thought of anything beyond that. In them we see his life passing. He is trifling it away; but no matter. He might do more with it, perhaps; but *cui bono?* At the end of his summer touring he writes: "A little Bedfordshire — a little Northamptonshire — a little more folding of the hands — the same faces — the same fields — the same thoughts occurring at the same turns of road — this is all I have to tell of; nothing at all added — but the summer gone. My garden is covered with yellow and brown leaves; and a man is digging up the garden beds before my window, and will plant some roots and bulbs for next year. My parsons come and smoke with me." What age does the reader give to the author of this paragraph, so full of afternoon shadows? He was thirty-five.

But if he was an idle fellow, careful for

nothing, poor in spirit, contented to be the hindmost, devil or no devil, "reading a little, dreaming a little, playing a little, smoking a little," doing whatever he did "a little," he was not without a kind of faith in his own capacity. He knew, or believed that he knew, what he was good for. "I am a man of taste," he said more than once. If he could not write poetry, — taste being only "the feminine of genius," — he knew it when he saw it. He read books with his own eyes, not half so common or easy a trick as many would suppose. And having read a book in that unconventional way, it was by no means to be taken for granted that he would like it, though its author might be one of his dearest friends. And if he failed to like it, he seldom failed to say so. If he commended a book, — a new book, that is, — it was apt to be with a mixture of criticism. He cared little or nothing for flattery himself, and was magnanimous enough to assume (an enormous assumption) that literary workers in general were equally highminded. If one friend sends another a book of his own writing, the best course for the second man is merely to acknowledge its receipt, unless he has some fault to indicate! This he sets down quite simply as his belief and ordinary practice. It was the more comfortable way for both parties, he thought. Perhaps he thought, too, that it was the more conducive to habits of truthfulness. (Others might conclude that its most immediate and permanent effect would be to discourage the circulation of authors' copies.) If he considered Mr. Lowell's odes to lack wings, he told Mr. Lowell so. If his taste was offended by the style of the "Moosehead Journal" ("too clever by half"), he told Mr. Lowell of that also. Why not? Great men did not resent truth-speaking, but were thankful for it. He was full of wonder and sorrow when he saw Tennyson — who had stopped at Woodbridge for a day to visit him, after a separation of twenty years — fretted by the "Quarterly's" unfavorable comments. If Tennyson had lived an active life, like Scott and Shakespeare, he would have done more and talked about it less. He recalls Scott's saying to Lockhart, "You know that I don't care a curse about what I write;" and he believed that it was not far otherwise with Shakespeare. "Even old Wordsworth, wrapt up in his mountain mists, and proud as he was, was above all this vain disquietude." If a man is not greater than the greatest things he does, the less said about him and them the better. His work should drop from him like fruit from a tree. Henceforth let the world look after it, if it is worth looking after. The tree should have other business.

To say that FitzGerald lived in accordance with his own doctrine in this regard is to say that he lived like a man of dignity and high self-respect, — like an old-fashioned man, — sometimes called a gentleman, — one is tempted to say: a man who would cut off his hand sooner than solicit a vote, or angle for a compliment, or whimper over a criticism. Old-fashioned he certainly was, — old-fashioned and conservative. He liked old books, old music, old places, old friends. The adjective is constantly on the point of his pen as a word of endearment: "old Alfred," "old Thackeray," "old Spedding" — "dear old

Jem." So, writing to Mrs. Kemble from the seacoast, he says, "Why it happens that I so often write to you from here, I scarce know; only that one comes with few books, perhaps, and the sea somehow talks to one of old things;" which was not an unhandsome tribute to an old friend, though the old friend was a woman. He was a "little Englander," as the word is now. For a nation, as for an individual, great estates were, he thought, more a trouble than a blessing. "Once more I say, would we were a little, peaceful, unambitious, trading nation, like — the Dutch!" Men of taste are naturally conservatives and moderates.

Not that FitzGerald was too nice for the world he lived in. His carelessness about dress, his contentment with mean lodgings, and his liking for the plainest and homeliest service and companionship have already been touched upon. Even in the matter of reading, while he held pretty strictly to the classics (not meaning the Greek and the Latin in particular), he cherished one bit of freakishness: a great fondness for the " Newgate Calendar"! "I don't ever wish to see and hear these things tried; but when they are in print, I like to sit in court then, and see the judges, counsel, prisoners, crowd; hear the lawyers' objections, the murmur in the court, etc." So he writes to his friend Allen, at fifty-six. And the passion remained with him, as most things do that are part of a man's life at fifty odd; for fourteen years later he writes to Mrs. Kemble, as of a matter well understood among his friends: "I like, you know, a good murder; but in its place —

'The charge is prepared; the lawyers are met —
The judges all ranged, a terrible show.'"[1]

It may be that on this point he was not so very eccentric. Certainly our newspaper editors give the general public credit for having a reasonably good appetite for capital cases. And FitzGerald's weakness — if it was a weakness — is curiously matched by what we are told of another eminent translator, the man to whom we

[1] In a letter to his friend Pollock he says: "To-morrow I am going to one of my great treats, namely, the Assizes at Ipswich: where I shall see little Voltaire Jervis, and old Parke, who I trust will have the gout, he bears it so Christianly."

owe our English Plato and Thucydides. A shy student, Mr. Tollemache says, happened to sit next to Jowett at dinner, and having hard work to maintain the conversation, as such men often had, in Jowett's unresponsive company, stumbled upon the subject of murder. "To his surprise the Master rose to the bait, mentioned some *causes célèbres*, and dropped all formality." Naturally the young Oxonian was surprised; but when he spoke of the incident to a man who knew the Master of Balliol better than he, the latter said, "If you can get Jowett to talk of murders, he will go off like a house on fire."

There is something of the savage ancestor in all of us. We are wrong, perhaps, to feel astonished that men of the cloister, studious men, never called upon to kill so much as a superfluous kitten, should find an agreeable excitement in a dramatic, second-hand tickling of certain half-dormant sensibilities. If it is ghastly good fun to read of murder in Scott or Dumas, why not in the "Newgate Calendar"? Who knows how many tender-hearted, white-handed scholars would enjoy the spectacle of a prize fight, if only the amusement were a few shades more respectable in the public eye? And how long is it since we saw college men falling over one another in a mad rush to enlist for battle, every one in a fever of anxiety lest he should be too late, and so be debarred from the unusual pleasure of killing and being killed?

No! When FitzGerald called himself a man of taste, he did not mean to confess himself an intellectual prig, with a schoolmaster's eye for petty failings and a super-refined disrelish for everything short of perfection. As for perfection, indeed, he did not much expect it, whether in human beings or in their works; and when he found it, he did not always like it. He thought some other things were better. He preferred genius to art: that is to say, he enjoyed high qualities, though accompanied by defects, better than lower qualities cultivated to a state of flawlessness. "The grandest things," he believed, "do not depend on delicate finish." Thus in poetry he admired a score of Béranger's almost perfect songs, but would have given them all for a score of Burns's couplets, stanzas, or single lines scattered among "his quite *im*perfect lyrics." Burns had so much more genius, so much more inspiration. In the same way FitzGerald had little patience with some perfect novels,— with Miss Austen's, to be more specific. They *were* perfect; yes, he had no thought of denying that; but they did not interest him. Even Trollope's were more to his mind, with all their caricature and carelessness. Miss Austen is "capital as far as she goes; but she never goes out of the parlor." "If Magnus Troil, or Jack Bunce, or even one of Fielding's brutes, would but dash in upon the gentility and swear a round oath or two!" Cowell, he adds, reads Miss Austen at night after his Sanskrit studies. "It composes him, like gruel."

There is no doubt of it, FitzGerald was old-fashioned, especially as a novel-reader. He doted on Clarissa Harlowe, "that wonderful and aggravating Clarissa Harlowe," and he read Dickens. "A little Shakespeare — a cockney Shakespeare, if you will . . . a piece of pure genius." So he breaks out after a chapter of Copperfield. "I have been sunning myself in Dickens," he says at another time. A pretty compliment that, for any man. It is good to hear his praise of Scott. Even those who can no longer abide that romancer themselves—for there are such, unaccountable as the fact may seem to happier men—may well feel a touch of warmth at FitzGerald's fire. He read fiction — as he read everything else — for pleasure; and in English no other fiction pleased him so much, taking the years together, as Sir Walter's. In 1871 he has been reading "The Pirate" again. He knows it is not one of the best, but he is glad to find how much he likes it; nay, that is below the mark, how he "wonders and delights in it." "With all its faults, often mere carelessness, what a broad Shakespearean daylight over it all, and all with no effort." He finished it with sadness, thinking he might never read it again.

And as he was always reading Scott, and as often praising him, so he was always reading and praising Don Quixote. In 1867 he has been on his yacht. "I have had Don Quixote, Boccaccio, and my dear Sophocles (once more) for company on board: the first of these so delightful that I got to love the very dictionary in which I had to look out the words: yes, and often the same words over and over again. The book really seemed to me the most delightful of all books: Boccaccio delightful too, but millions of miles behind; in fact, a whole planet away." In 1876 his mind is the same. "I have taken refuge from the Eastern Question in Boccaccio. . . . I suppose one must read this in Italian as my dear Don in Spanish: the language of each fitting the subject 'like a glove.' But there is nothing to come up to the Don and his Man."

Bookishness of this affectionate, enthusiastic sort, constantly recurring, would be enough of itself to give the letters a welcome; for every reader loves to hear books praised at first hand, the man rather than the critic speaking, even though they be such as lie outside the too narrow limits of his own appreciation. Happiness is contagious, and it is better than nothing, as was said just now, to warm one's self at another's fire.

FitzGerald's relations with books (with *his* books) were those of a lover. He can never say all he feels about Virgil. Horace he is unable to care about, in spite of his good sense, elegance, and occasional force. "He never made my eyes wet as Virgil does." When he reads "Comus" and "Lycidas," even at seventy, it is "with wonder and a sort of awe." Surely he was a man of taste; born to be an appreciator of other men's good work.

And because he was a man of taste, — or partly for that reason, — his praise, even in its warmest and most personal expression (like the words just quoted about Virgil), has not only no taint of affectation, but no suggestion of sentimentality. With him, as with all healthy souls, feeling was a matter of moments; it came in jets, not in a stream; and its outgiving was always with a note of unconsciousness, of deep and absolute sincerity. His life, inward and outward, was pitched in a low key. He never complained, let what would happen; he had too much of "old Omar's consolation" for that (too much fatalism, that is); his own weaknesses, even, he took as they were; why regret what was past mending? but his prevailing mood was anything but rhapsodical. All the more effective, therefore, are the outbursts — frequent, but never more than a sentence or two together — in which he utters himself touching those best of all companions, his "friends on the shelf."

The most striking instance of this affectionate absorption, this falling in love with a book, as one cannot help calling it, occurred in the last decade of his life. In the summer of 1875, when his health seemed to be failing, and he was beginning, as he said, to "smell the ground," he suddenly became enamored of Madame de Sévigné. Till then, in spite of his favorite Sainte-Beuve, he had kept aloof from her, repelled by her perpetual harping on her daughter. Now he finds that "it is all genuine, and the same intense feeling expressed in a hundred natural yet graceful ways; and beside all this such good sense, good feeling, humor, love of books and country life, as makes her certainly the queen of all letter-writers."

The next spring he wishes he had the "Go" in him; he would visit his dear Sévigné's Rochers, as he would Abbotsford and Stratford. The " fine creature," much more alive to him than most friends, has been his companion at the seashore. She now occupies Montaigne's place, and worthily; "she herself a lover of Montaigne, and with a spice of his free thought and speech in her." He sometimes laments not having known her before; but reflects that "perhaps such an acquaintance comes in best to cheer one toward the end." Henceforward, year after year, in spring especially, he talks of the dear lady's charms. "My blessed Sévigné," "my dear old Sévigné," he calls her; "welcome as the flowers of May." Like the best of Scott's characters, she is real and present to him. "When my oracle last night was reading to me of Dandie Dinmont's blessed visit to Bertram in Portanferry gaol, I said — 'I know it's Dandie, and I should n't be at all surprised to see him come into this room.' No — no more than — Madame de Sévigné! I suppose it is scarce right to live so among shadows; but after near seventy years so passed, *que voulez-vous?*" One thinks of what Emerson said, that there is creative reading as well as creative writing.

As is true of all readers, every kind of human capacity being limited, FitzGerald found many likely books lying mysteriously outside the range of his sympathies. He loved Longfellow (and so "could not call him Mister") and admired Emerson (with qualifications — "I don't like the 'Humble Bee,' and won't like the 'Humble Bee'"); and he delighted in Lowell (the critical essays), and "rather loved" Holmes; but he "could never take to that man of true genius, Hawthorne." "I will have another shot," he said. But it was useless. He confesses his failure to Professor Norton. "I feel sure the fault must be mine, as I feel about Goethe, who is yet a sealed book to me." He expects to "die ungoethed, so far as poetry goes." He supposes there is a screw loose in him on this point. Again he writes: "I have failed in another attempt at 'Gil Blas.' I believe I see its easy grace, humor, etc. But it is (like La Fontaine) too thin a wine for me: all sparkling with little adventures, but no one to care about; no color, no breadth, like my dear Don, whom I shall return to forthwith." Happy reader, who could give so pretty a reason for the want of faith that was in him. If he lacked patience to write formal criticism, he had the neatest kind of knack at critical *obiter dicta*.

Books were his best friends; or, if that be too much to say, they were the ones that he liked best to have about him. As for human intimates, — well, it is hard to know how to express it, but he seemed, especially as he grew older, not to crave very much of their society. He loved to write to them, — not too often, lest they should be troubled about replying, — but he would never visit them; and what is stranger, he cared little, nay, he almost dreaded, to have them visit him. His house he devoted to his nieces, for such part of the year as they chose to occupy it, reserving but one room to himself. This serves for "parlor, bedroom and all," he tells Mrs. Kemble; "which I really prefer, as it reminds me of the cabin of my dear little ship — mine no more." Still the house is large enough. If any of his friends,

Tennyson, Spedding, Carlyle, Mr. Lowell, Mr. Norton, or who not, should happen to be in the neighborhood, he would be delighted, truly delighted, to see them; but none of them must ever undertake the journey on purpose. He could n't render it worth their while, and it would really make him unhappy. He was never in danger of forgetting them, and he had no fear of their forgetting him. If they suffered, he suffered with them. If one of them died, he wrote of him in the tenderest and most poignant strain.

In January, 1864, all his letters are full of Thackeray, whose death had occurred on the day before Christmas. He sits "moping about him," reading his books and the few of his letters that he has preserved. He writes to Laurence: "I am surprised almost to find how much I am thinking of him: so little as I had seen him for the last ten years; not once for the last five. I had been told — by you, for one — that he was spoiled. I am glad therefore that I have scarce seen him since he was 'old Thackeray.' I keep reading his 'Newcomes' of nights, and as it were hear him saying so much of it; and it seems to me as if he might be coming up my stairs, and about to come (singing) into my room, as in old Charlotte Street thirty years ago." [1]

Hear him again as he writes of Spedding, the wisest man he has ever known, "a Socrates in life and in death," who has been run over by a cab in London, and is dying at the hospital: "My dear old Spedding, though I have not seen him these twenty years and more, and probably should never see him again; but he lives, his old self, in my heart of hearts; and all I hear of him does but embellish the recollection of him, if it could be embellished; for he is but the same that he was from a boy, all that is best in heart and head, a man that would be incredible had one not known him." And when all is over, and Laurence sends him tidings of the event, this is his answer: "It was very, very good of you to think of writing to me at all on

[1] In connection with which it is good to remember that when Thackeray, not long before he died, was asked by his daughter which of his old friends he had loved most, he replied, "Why, dear old Fitz, to be sure." After FitzGerald's death Tennyson wrote of him: "I had no truer friend: he was one of the kindliest of men, and I have never known one of so fine and delicate a wit."

EDWARD FITZGERALD

this occasion: much more, writing to me so fully, almost more fully than I dared at first to read: though all so delicately and as you always write. It is over! I shall not write about it. He was all you say." How perfect! And how it goes to the quick!

Not for want of heart, surely, did such a man choose the companionship of books rather than of his fellows. He was born to be a solitary, or believed that he was; at all events, it was too late now for him to be anything else. Whether nature or he had made his bed, it was made, and henceforth he must lie in it. "Twenty years' solitude," he says to Mrs. Kemble, "makes me very shy." And he writes to Sir Frederick Pollock, who has proposed to visit him, that he feels nervous at the prospect of meeting old friends, "after all these years." He fears they will not find him in person what he is by letter. Every recluse knows that trouble. With books it was another story. In their presence he felt no misgivings, no palsying diffidence. They would never expect of him what he could not render, nor find him altered from his old self. If he happened to be awkward or dull, as he often was, they would never know it. And really, with them on his shelves, and with his habit of living by himself, he did not need intellectual society,—just a few commonplace, kindly, more or less sensible bodies to speak with in a neighborly way about the weather, the crops, or the day's events, and to play cards with of an evening. He was one of the fortunates—or unfortunates—who have a "talent for dullness." The word is his own. "I really do like to sit in this doleful place with a good fire, a cat and dog on the rug, and an old woman in the kitchen." He reveled in the pleasures of memory. He loved his friends as they were years ago,—"old Thackeray," "old Jem," "old Alfred,"—and only hoped they would love him in the same manner.

So his letters are full of the books he has been reading, rather than of the people he has been talking with. But what of his own books, especially of the one that has made him famous? About that, it must be said at once, the correspondence tells comparatively little. His Persian studies were only an episode in his life, interesting enough at the time, but not a continuous passion, like, for instance, his reading of Crabbe, and his long persisted in — never relinquished — attempt to secure for that half-forgotten Suffolk poet the honor rightfully belonging to him. Concerning that pious attempt, as concerning a possible republication of some of his translations from the Spanish and the Greek, he left directions with his literary executor; but not a word about Omar Khayyám.

The whole Persian business, indeed, if one may speak of it so, appears to have been largely a matter of friendship, or at least to have been begun as such. Cowell had become absorbed in that language, and enticed his old Spanish pupil to follow him. The first mention of the subject to be found in the published letters occurs in 1853. FitzGerald has ordered Eastwick's "Gulistan:" "for I believe I shall potter out so much Persian." Two months afterward he writes to Frederic Tennyson: "I amuse myself with poking out some Persian which E. Cowell would inaugurate me with. I go on with it because it is a point in common with him, and enables us to study a little together." Friendly feeling has served the world many a good turn, but rarely a better one than this.

Three or four years later comes the first reference to Omar. "Old Omar," he says, "rings like true metal." Now he is translating the quatrains, though he has little to say about them. He finds it amusing to "take what liberties he likes with these Persians," who, he thinks, are not poets enough to frighten one from so doing. On a 1st of July he writes: "June over! A thing I think of with Omar-like sorrow." Then he is preparing to send some of the more innocent of the quatrains to "Fraser's Magazine," the editor of which has asked him for a contribution. He has begun to look upon Omar as rather more his property than Cowell's. "He and I are more akin, are we not?" he writes to his teacher. "You see all his beauty, but you don't feel *with* him in some respects as I do." He is taking all pains, not for literalness, but to make the thing *live*. It *must* live; if not with Omar's life, why, then, with the translator's. And live it did, and does, —

"The rose of Iran on an English stock."

The Fraser story is well known,—a classical example of the rejection of a future classic. The editor took the manuscript, but kept it in its pigeonhole ("Thou knowest not which shall prosper" being as true a text for editors as for other men— "Sir," said Doctor Johnson, "a fallible being will fail somewhere"), and at last FitzGerald asked it back, added something to it, and printed it anonymously. This was in 1859. He gave one copy to Cowell (who "was naturally alarmed at it; he being a very religious man"), one copy to George Borrow, and one — a good while afterward—to "old Donne." Some copies he kept for himself. The remainder, two hundred, more or less, he presented to Mr. Quaritch, who had printed them for him, and who worked them off upon his customers, as best he could, mostly at two cents apiece.

In the course of the next few years three other editions were printed — all anonymously—for the sake of alterations and additions (a man of taste is sure to be a patient reviser), but there is next to nothing about them in the letters. No one cares for such things, the translator says. He hardly knows why he prints them, only that he likes to make an end of the matter. So he writes to Cowell. As for the rest of his correspondents, they are more likely to be interested in other things,—his garden, his boat, his reading. By 1863 he is pretty well tired of everything Persian. "Oh dear," he says to his teacher, "when I look at Homer, Dante and Virgil, Æschylus, Shakespeare, etc., those Orientals look — silly! Don't resent my saying so. *Don't* they?" An English masterpiece had been made, but neither the maker of it nor any one else had yet suspected the fact.

The merits of the work seem to have been first publicly recognized in 1869 by Mr. Charles Eliot Norton, in an article contributed to the "North American Review." "The work of a poet inspired by the work of a poet," he pronounces it; "not a copy, but a reproduction, not a translation, but the redelivery of a poetic inspiration." "There is probably nothing in the mass of English translations or reproductions of the poetry of the East to be compared with this little volume in

EDWARD FITZGERALD

point of value as *English* poetry. In the strength of rhythmical structure, in force of expression, in musical modulation, and in mastery of language, the external character of the verse corresponds with the still rarer qualities of imagination and of spiritual discernment which it displays."

It would be pleasant to know how appreciation of this kind, coming unexpectedly from a stranger over seas, affected the still anonymous, obscurity-loving translator; but if he ever read it, or, having read it, said anything about it, the letters make no sign. He and his work were still comfortably obscure. His old friend Carlyle heard not a word about the matter till 1873, when Professor Norton, who meanwhile had somehow discovered the name of the man he had been praising, mentioned the poem to him, and insisted upon giving him a copy. Carlyle, much pleased, at once wrote to FitzGerald a letter which was undoubtedly meant to be very kind and handsome, but which, read in the light of the present, sounds a little perfunctory, and even a bit patronizing. The translation, he says, is a "meritorious and successful performance." We can almost fancy that we are listening to a good-natured but truthful man who feels it his duty to speak well of a pretty good composition written by a fairly bright grammar school boy.

It was all one to FitzGerald. Perhaps he thought the compliment as good as he deserved. He was getting old — as he had been doing for the last twenty-five years. Persian poetry was little or nothing to him now — "a ten years' dream." The fruit had dropped from the tree; let the earth care for it. So he returns to his Crabbe, to Sainte-Beuve, to Madame de Sévigné, to Don Quixote, to Wesley's Journal, and the rest. Such little time as he has to live, he will live quietly. And ten years afterward, when he died, — suddenly, as he had always hoped, — some one put on his gravestone that most Omaric of Scripture texts, "It is He that hath made us, and not we ourselves." Perhaps the words were of his own choosing. Certainly no others could have suited him so well. If he had been eccentric, idle, unambitious, ease-loving, incapable, a pitcher "leaning all awry," he had been what the Potter made him.

> "The Ball no question makes of Ayes and Noes,
> But Here or There as strikes the Player goes;
> And He that tossed you down into the Field,
> He knows about it all — HE knows — HE knows!"

Since his death his fame has increased mightily. All the world reads Omar Khayyám and praises FitzGerald. "His strange genius, so fitfully and coyly revealed, has given a new quality to English verse, almost all recent manifestations of which it pervades." So says one of the later historians of our nineteenth century literature. And the man himself thought he had done nothing! Truly the race is not to the swift.

> "Behold the Grace of Allah comes and goes
> As to Itself is good: and no one knows
> Which way it turns: in that mysterious Court
> Not he most finds who furthest travels for 't,
> For one may crawl upon his knees Life-long,
> And yet may never reach, or all go wrong:
> Another just arriving at the Place
> He toiled for, and — the Door shut in his Face:
> Whereas Another, scarcely gone a Stride,
> And suddenly — Behold he is inside!"

THOREAU

THOREAU

"Whoever will do his own work aright will find that his first lesson is to know what he is, and that which is proper to himself; and whoever rightly understands himself will never mistake another man's work for his own, but will love and improve himself above all other things, will refuse superfluous employments, and reject all unprofitable thoughts and propositions."

MONTAIGNE.

It lay at the root of Thoreau's peculiarity that he insisted upon being himself. Having certain opinions, he held them; having certain tastes, he encouraged them; having a certain faculty, he made the most of it: all of which, natural and reasonable as it may sound, is as far as possible from what is expected of the average citizen, who may be almost anything he will, to be sure, if he will first observe the golden rule of good society, to be "like other folks." Society is still a kind of self-constituted militia, a mutual protective association,— an army, in short; and in an army, as everybody knows, the first duty of man is to keep step.

What made matters worse in Thoreau's case was, that his tastes and opinions, on which he so stoutly insisted, were in themselves far out of the common. Not only would he be himself, enough, under present conditions, to make almost any man an oddity, but the "himself" was essentially a very queer person. He liked solitude; in other words, he liked to think. He loved the society of trees and all manner of growing things. He found fellowship in them, they were of his kin; which is not at all the same as to say that he enjoyed looking at them as objects of beauty. He lived in a world of his own, a world of ideas, and was strangely indifferent to much that other men found absorbing. He could get along without a daily newspaper, but not without a daily walk. He spent hours and hours of honest daylight in what looked for all the world like idleness; and he did it industriously and on principle. He was more anxious to live well — according to an inward standard of his own — than to lodge well, or to dress well, or to stand well with his townsmen. A good name, even, was relatively unimportant. He found easy sundry New Testament scriptures which the church would still be stumbling over, only that it has long since worn a smooth path round them.

He set a low value on money. It *might* be of service to him, he once confessed, underscoring the doubt, but in general he accepted poverty as the better part. "We are often reminded," he said, "that if there were bestowed on us the wealth of Crœsus, our aims must still be the same, and our means essentially the same." Houses and lands, even, as he considered them, were often no better than incumbrances. Some of his well-to-do, highly respected, self-satisfied neighbors were as good as in prison, he thought. In what sense were men to be called free, if their "property" had put them under bonds to stay in such and such a place and do only such and such things? Life was more than meat, as he reckoned, and having trained himself to "strict business habits" (his own words), he did not believe in swapping a better thing for a poorer one. To him it was amazing that hard-headed, sensible men should stand at a desk the greater part of their days, and "glimmer and rust, and finally go out there." "If they *know* anything," he exclaimed, "what under the sun do they do that for?" He speaks as if the question were unanswerable; but no doubt many readers will find it easy enough, the only real difficulty being a deplorable scarcity of desks. For Thoreau's part, at any rate, other men might save dollars if they would; he meant to save his soul. It should not glimmer and rust and go out, if a manly endeavor was good for anything. And he saved it. To the end he kept it alive; and though he died young, he lived a long life and did a long life's work, and what is more to the present purpose, he left behind him a long memory.

His economies, which were so many and so rigorous, were worthy of a man. In kind, they were such as any man must practice who, having a task assigned him, is set upon doing it. If the river is to run the mill, it must contract itself. The law is general. To make sure of the best we must put away not only whatever is bad, but many things that of themselves are good, — a right hand, if need be, or a right eye, said one of old. For the artist, indeed, as for the saint, — for all seekers after perfection, that is, — the good and the best are often the most uncompromising of opposites, by no means to be entertained under the same roof. Manage it as we will, to receive one is to dismiss the other.

Rightly considered, Thoreau's singularity consisted, not in his lodging in a cabin, nor in his wearing coarse clothes, nor in his non-observance of so-called social amenities, nor even in his passion for the wild, but in his view of the world and of his own place in it. He was a poet-naturalist, an idealist, an individualist, a transcendental philosopher, what you will; but first of all he was a prophet. "I am the voice of one crying in the wilderness," he might have said; and the locusts and wild honey followed as things of course. It followed, also, that the fathers neglected him, — stoning having gone out of fashion, — and the children garnish his sepulchre. A prophet is a very worthy person — after he is dead. Then come biographies, eulogies, and new editions of his works, including his journals and private letters. Fame is a plant that blossoms on graves; as a manual of such botany might say, "a late-flowering perennial, nowhere common, to be looked for in old cemeteries."

A prophet, a writer, a student of nature: this was Thoreau, and the three were one.

He preached faith, simplicity, devotion to the ideal; and with all a prophet's freedom he denounced everything antagonistic, to these. He was not one of those nice people who are contented to speak handsomely of God and say nothing about the devil. It was not in his nature to halt between two opinions. He could always say yes or no — especially no. As was said of Pascal, there were no middle terms in his philosophy.

Withal, no man was more of a believer and less of a skeptic. Faith and hope, "infinite expectation," were his daily breath. Charity was his, also, but less conspicuously, and after a pattern of his own, philanthropy, as he saw it practiced, being one of his prime aversions. He knew not the meaning of pessimism. The world was good. "I am grateful for what I am and

have. My thanksgiving is perpetual." To
the final hour existence was a boon to him.
"For joy I could embrace the earth,"
he declared, though he seldom indulged
himself in emotional expression; "I shall
delight to be buried in it." "It was not
possible to be sad in his presence," said
his sister, speaking of his last illness. His
may have been "a solitary and critical
way of living," to quote Emerson's careful
phrase, but in his work there is little trace of
anything morbid or unwholesome. Some
who might hesitate to rank themselves
among his disciples keep by them a copy of
"Walden," or the "Week," to dip into for
refreshment and invigoration when life runs
low and desire begins to fail. Readers of
this kind please him better, we may guess,
if he knows of them, than those who skim
his pages for the natural history and the
scenery. Such is the fate of prophets. The
fulminations and entreaties of Isaiah are
now highly recommended as specimens of
Oriental *belles-lettres*. Yet worse things may
befall a man than to be partially appreciated. As Thoreau himself said: "It is the
characteristic of great poems that they will

yield of their sense in due proportion to the hasty and the deliberate reader. To the practical they will be common sense, and to the wise wisdom; as either the traveler may wet his lips, or an army may fill its water-casks at a full stream." His own was hardly a "full stream," perhaps; a mountain brook rather than one of the world's rivers; clear, cold, running from the spring, untainted by the swamp; less majestic than the Amazons, but not less unfailing, and for those who can climb, and who know the taste of purity, infinitely sweeter to drink from.

Simplicity of life and devotion to the ideal, the one a means to the other, — these he would preach, in season and, if possible, out of season. "Simplicity, simplicity, simplicity! I say, let your affairs be as two or three, and not a hundred or a thousand; instead of a million count half a dozen, and keep your accounts on your thumb-nail." This, which, after all, is nothing but the old doctrine of the one thing needful, — since it is one mark of a prophet that he deals not in novelties, but in truth, — all this spiritual economy is connected at the root with Thoreau's belief in free will, his vital assurance that the nobility or meanness of a man's life is committed largely to his own choice. He may waste it on the trivial, or spend it on the essential. There is "no more encouraging fact than the unquestionable ability of man to elevate his life by a conscious endeavor." And what a man is inwardly, that to *him* will the world be outwardly; his mood affects the very "quality of the day." Could anything be truer or more finely suggested? For himself, Thoreau was determined to get the goodness out of time as it passed. He refused to be hurried. The hour was too precious. "If the bell rings, why should we run?" Neither would he knowingly take up with a second-best, or be put off with a sham, — as if there were nothing real. He would not "drive a nail into mere lath and plastering," he declared. Such a deed would keep him awake nights. A very reasonable and practical kind of doctrine, certainly, whether it be called transcendentalism or common sense. Perhaps we discredit it with a long word by way of refusing the obligation it would lay us under.

And possibly it is for a similar reason that the world in general has agreed to regard Thoreau not as a preacher of righteousness, but as an interpreter of nature. For those who have settled down to take things as they are, having knocked under and gone with the stream, in Thoreau's language, it is pleasanter to read of beds of water-lilies flashing open at sunrise, or of a squirrel's pranks upon a bough, than of daily aspiration after an ideal excellence. Whatever the reason, Thoreau is to the many a man who lived out of doors, and wrote of outdoor things.

His attainments as a naturalist have been by turns exaggerated and belittled, one extreme following naturally upon the other. As for the exaggeration, nothing else was to be expected, things being as they were. It is what happens in every such case. If a man knows some of the birds, his neighbors, who know none of them, celebrate him at once as an ornithologist. If he is reputed to "analyze" flowers, — pull them to pieces under a pocket-lens, and by means of a key find out their polysyllabic names, — he straightway becomes famous as a botanist; all of which is a little as if the ticket-seller and the grocer's clerk should be hailed as financiers because of their facility in making change.

Thoreau knew his local fauna and flora after a method of his own, a method which, for lack of a better word, may be called sympathetic. Nobody was ever more successful in getting inside of a bird; and that, from his point of view and for his purpose, — and not less for ours who read him, — was the one important thing. After that it mattered little if some of his flying neighbors escaped his notice altogether, while others led him a vain chase year after year, and are still, in his published journals, a puzzle to readers. Who knows what his night warbler was, or, with certainty, his seringo bird? The latter, indeed, a native of his own Concord hay-fields, he seems to have been pretty well acquainted with as a bird; its song was familiar to him, and less frequently he caught sight of the singer itself perched upon a fence-post or threading its way through the grass; but he had found no means of ascertaining its name, and so was driven to the primitive expedient of christening it with an invention of his own. His description of its appearance and notes leaves us in no great doubt as to its identity; probably it was the savanna sparrow; but how completely in the dark he himself was upon this point may be gathered from an entry in his journal of 1854. He had gone to Nantucket, in late December, and there saw, running along the ruts, flocks of "a gray, bunting-like bird about the size of the snow-bunting. Can it be the seaside finch," he asks, "or the savanna sparrow, or the shore lark?" Savanna sparrow, or shore lark! A Baldwin apple, or a russet! But what then? There are gaps in every scholar's knowledge, and the man who has "named *all* the birds without a gun" is yet to be heard from. It is fair to remind ourselves, also, that Thoreau's studies in this line were pursued under limitations and disadvantages to which the amateur of our later day is happily a stranger. Ornithologically, it is a long time since Thoreau's death, though it is less than forty-five years.

If any be disposed to insist, as some

have insisted, that he made no discoveries
(he discovered a new way of writing about
nature, for one thing), and was more curious than scientific in his spirit and method
as an observer, it is perhaps sufficient to
reply that he cultivated his own field. From
first to last he refused the claims of science, — whether rightly or wrongly is not
here in question, — and with the exception
of one or two brief essays wrote nothing
directly upon natural history. He worshiped Nature, even while he played the
spy upon her, fearing her enchantments
and "looking at her with the side of his
eye." Run over the titles of his books:
"A Week on the Concord and Merrimack
Rivers," "Walden," "The Maine Woods,"
"Cape Cod," "A Yankee in Canada,"
"Excursions." The first two are studies
in high and plain living, — practical philosophy, spiritual economy, the right use
of society and solitude, books and nature.
The rest are narratives of travel, with a
record of what the traveler saw and thought
and felt. In "Excursions," to be sure, there
is an early paper on "The Natural History of Massachusetts," to which, by strain-

ing a point, we may add one on "The Succession of Forest Trees," another on "Autumnal Tints," and still another on "Wild Apples." Elsewhere, though the landscape is sure to be carefully studied, it is always a landscape with figures. In truth, while he wrote so much of outward nature, and so often seemed to find his fellow-mortals no better than intruders upon the scene, his real subject was man. "Man is all in all," he says; "Nature nothing but as she draws him out and reflects him." And again he said, "Any affecting human event may blind our eyes to natural objects."

The latter sentence was written shortly after the death of John Brown, in whose fate Thoreau had been so completely absorbed that his old Concord world, when he came back to it, had almost a foreign look to him, and he remarked with a start of surprise that the little grebe was still diving in the river. With all his devotion to nature and philosophy, it was the "human event" that really concerned him. But of course he had ideas of his own as to what constituted an event. As for men's so-called affairs, and all that passes current under the name of news, nothing could be less eventful; for all such things he could never sufficiently express his contempt. "In proportion as our inward life fails," he says, "we go more constantly and desperately to the post-office." And he adds, in that peculiarly airy manner of his to which one is tempted sometimes to apply the old Yankee adjective "toplofty," "I would not run round the corner to see the world blow up." After which, the reader whose bump of incuriosity is less highly developed may console himself by remembering that when a powder-mill blew up in the next town, Thoreau, hearing the noise, ran downstairs, jumped into a wagon, and drove post-haste to the scene of the disaster. So true is it that it is

> "the most difficult of tasks to keep
> Heights which the soul is competent to gain."

Careful economist as Thoreau was, bravely as he trusted his own intuitions and kept to his own path, much as he preached simplicity and heroically as he practiced it, he shared the common lot and fell short of his own ideal. Life is never quite so simple as he attempted to make it, and he, like other men, was conscious of a divided mind. He had by nature a bias toward the investigation of natural phenomena, a passion for particulars, which, if he had been less a poet and philosopher, might have made him a man of science. He knew it, and was inwardly chafed by it. Perhaps it was because of this chafing that he fell into the habit of speaking so almost spitefully of science and scientific men. Not to lay stress upon his frequent paradoxes about the superiority of superstition to knowledge, the advantages of astrology over astronomy, the slight importance of precision in matters of detail ("I can afford to be inaccurate"), — to say nothing of these things, which, taken as they were meant, are not without a measure of truth, and with which no lover of Thoreau will be much disposed to quarrel (those who cannot abide the nudge of a paradox or an inch or two of exaggeration may as well let him alone), it is plain that in certain moods, especially in his later years, his own semi-scientific researches were felt to be a hindrance to the play of his higher faculties. "It is impossible for the same person to see things from the poet's point of view and that of the man of science," he writes in 1842. "Man cannot afford to be a naturalist," he says again, in 1853. "I feel that I am dissipated by so many observations. . . . Oh, for a little Lethe!" And a week afterward he falls into the same strain, in a tone of reminiscence that is of the very rarest with him. "Ah, those youthful days," he breaks out, "are they never to return? when the walker does not too enviously observe particulars, but sees, hears, scents, tastes, and feels only himself, the phenomena that showed themselves in him, his expanding body, his intellect and heart. No worm or insect, quadruped or bird, confined his view, but the unbounded universe was his. A bird has now become a mote in his eye." What devotee of natural science, if he be also a man of sensibility and imagination, does not feel the sincerity of this cry?

But having delivered himself thus passionately, what does the diarist set down next? Without a break he goes on: "Dug into what I take to be a woodchuck's burrow in the low knoll below the cliffs. It was in the side of the hill, and sloped gently downward at first diagonally into the hill about five feet, perhaps westerly, then turned and ran north about three feet, then northwest further into the hill four feet, then north again four feet, then northeast I know not how far, the last five feet, perhaps, ascending," — with as much more of the same tenor and equally detailed. A laughable paragraph, surely, to follow a lament over a too envious observation of particulars; with its "perhaps" four times repeated, its five feet westerly, three feet northerly, and so on, like a conveyancer's description of a wood-lot: and all about a hole in the ground, which he "took to be" a woodchuck's burrow!

In vain shall a man bestir himself to run away from his own instincts. In vain, in such a warfare, shall he trust to the freedom of the will. Happily for himself, and happily for the world, Thoreau, though he "could not afford to be a naturalist," could never cease from his "too envious observation."

By inclination and habit he liked to see and do things for himself, as if they had never been seen or done before. That was one mark of his individualistic temper, not to say a chief mark of his genius. He describes in his journal an experiment in making sugar from the sap of red maple trees. Here, too, he goes into the minutest details, not omitting the size of the holes he bored and the frequency with which the drops fell, — about as fast as his pulse beat. His father, he mentions (the son was then forty years old), chided him for wasting his time. There was no occasion for the experiment, the father thought; it was well known that the thing could be done; and as for the sugar, it could be bought cheaper at the village shop. "He said it took me from my studies," the journal records. "I said that I made it my study, and felt as if I had been to a university." If fault-finding is in order, an individualist prefers to administer it on his own account. One remembers Thoreau's characteristic declaration that he had never received the first word of valuable counsel from any of his elders. In the present instance, surely, as much as this must be said for him, — that by habits of this unpractical-seeming kind knowledge is made peculiarly one's own, and, old or new, keeps something of the freshness of discovery upon it. The critic may smile, but even he will not dispute the charm of writing done in such a spirit, — the very spirit in which the old books were written, in the childhood of the world.

Even the edibility of white-oak acorns affected Thoreau, at the age of forty, as a new fact. So far as his feeling about it was concerned, the fruit might have been that morning created. "The whole world is sweeter" to him for having "discovered" it. "To have found two Indian gouges and tasted sweet acorns, is it not enough for one afternoon?" he asks himself. And the next day, shrewd economist and exaggerator that he is, he tries his new dainty again, and behold, a second discovery: the acorns "appear to dry sweet!" One need not be a critic, but only a homely-witted, country-bred Yankee, to smile at this. But indeed, it is a relief to be able to smile now and then at one who held himself so high and aloof, — "a Switzer on the edge of the glacier," as he called himself; who found no wisdom too lofty for him, no companionship quite lofty enough; and who, in his longing for something better than the best, could exclaim, "Give me a sentence which no intelligence can understand." Not that we feel any diminution of our respect or affection; but it pleases us to have met our Switzer for once on something near our own level. In an author, as in a friend, an amiable weakness, if there be strength enough behind it, is only another point of attraction.

As a writer, Thoreau is by himself. There are no other books like "Walden" and the "Week." The reader may like them or leave them (unless he is pretty sure of himself, he may be advised to try "Walden" first), he will find nowhere else the same combination of pure nature and austere philosophy. It is hard even to see with what to compare them, or to conceive of any one else as having written them. If Marcus Aurelius, with half his sweetness of temper eliminated, and something of sharpness, together with liberal measures of cool intellectuality, injected, could have been united with Gilbert White, rather less radically transformed, and if the resultant complex person had made it his business to write, we can perhaps imagine that his work would not have been in all respects unlike that of the sage of Walden; in saying which we have but taken a circuitous course back to our former position, that Thoreau was a man of his own kind.

He was an author from the beginning. Of that, as he said himself, he was never in doubt. His ceaseless observation of nature — which some have decried as lacking purpose and method — and his daily journal were deliberately chosen means to that end. "Here have I been these forty years learning the language of these fields that I may the better express myself." That was what he aimed at, let his subject be what it might, — to express *himself*.

Few writers have ever treated their work more seriously, or studied their art more industriously. He talked sometimes, to be sure, as if there were no art about it. To listen to him in such a mood, one might suppose that the fact and the thought were the only things to be considered, and that language followed of itself. Such was neither his belief nor his practice. But he was one of the fortunate ones who by taking pains can produce an effect of easiness; who can recast and recast a sentence, and in the end leave it looking as if it had dropped from a running pen. One of the fortunates, we say; for an air of innocent unconsciousness is as becoming in a sentence as in a face.

On this point a useful study in contrasts might be made between Thoreau and a man who gladly acknowledged him as one of his masters. "Upon me," says Robert Louis Stevenson, "this pure, narrow, sunnily ascetic Thoreau had exercised a great charm. I have scarce written ten sentences since I was introduced to him, but his influence might be somewhere detected by a close observer." The observer would need to be very close indeed, the majority of Stevensonians will think, but that, true or false, is nothing to the purpose here. Stevenson and Thoreau both made writing a lifelong study, and with exceedingly diverse results. The Scotchman's style is the finer, but then it is sometimes in danger of becoming *super*fine. We may not wish it different. Such work must be as it is. It could hardly be better without being worse, the writing of fine prose being always a question of compromises, a gain here for a loss there, a choice of imperfections; perfect prose being in fact impossible, except in the briefest snatches. But surely Stevenson's gift was not an absolute naturalness and transparency, such as lets the thought show through on the instant, and leaves the beauty of the verbal medium to catch the attention afterward, if the reader will. "For love of lovely words," an artist of Stevenson's temperament, however sound his theories, may sometimes find it hard to make a righteous choice between the music of an exquisite cadence and the pure expressiveness of a halting phrase. The author of "Walden" had his literary temptations, but not of this kind. Let the phrase halt, so long as it expressed a sturdy truth in sturdy fashion. As for that homely quality — "careless country talk" — which Thoreau prayed for, and in good measure received, it is questionable whether Stevenson ever sought it, though he would no doubt have assented to Thoreau's words: "Homeliness is almost as great a merit in a book as in a house, if the reader would abide there. It is next to beauty, and a very high art."

Thoreau, indeed, first as a spiritual economist, and next as an artist, had a natural relish for the common and the plain. Every landscape that was dreary enough, as he says of Cape Cod, had a certain beauty in his eyes. Whether in literature or in life, he preferred the beauty that is inherent, — the beauty of the thing itself. Ornament, beauty laid on, did not much attract him. Among persons, it was the wilder-seeming, the less tamed and cultivated, with whom he liked to converse, and whose sayings he oftenest recorded. Though they might be crabbed specimens, "run all to thorn and rind, and crowded out of shape by adverse circumstances, like the third chestnut in the burr," they were still what nature had made them. Even a crowd pleased him, if it was composed of the right materials, — that is to say, if it was rude enough. Thus he, a hermit, took pleasure in the autumnal cattle-show. With what a touch of affection he lays on the colors! "The wind goes hurrying down the country, gleaning every loose straw that is left in the fields, while every farmer lad, too, appears to scud before it,—having donned his best pea-jacket and pepper-and-salt waistcoat, his unbent trousers, outstanding rigging of duck, or kerseymere, or corduroy, and his furry hat withal, — to country fairs and cattle-shows, to that Rome among the villages where the treasures of the year are gathered. All the land over they go leaping the fences with their tough, idle palms, which have never learned to hang by their sides, amid the low of calves and the bleating of sheep, — Amos, Abner, Elnathan, Elbridge, —

'From steep pine-bearing mountains to the plain.'

I love these sons of earth, every mother's son of them." It is worth while to see the country's people, he thinks, and even the "supple vagabond," who is "sure to appear on the least rumor of such a gathering, and the next day to disappear, and go into his hole like the seventeen-year locust."

For the average (uninitiated) reader, be it said, there is nothing better in Thoreau than his thumb-nail sketches of humble, every-day humanity; as there is no part of his work, not even his denunciation of worldly conformity, or his picturing of nature's moods, which is done with more absolute good-will. A man need not be an idealist, a naturalist, or anything else out of the ordinary, to like the Canadian woodchopper, for example, cousin to the pine and the rock, who never was tired in his life, and, stranger still, sometimes acted as if he were "thinking for himself and expressing his own opinions;" or the old fisherman, always haunting the river in serene afternoons, and "almost rustling with the sedge;" or the Cape Cod wrecker, whose face was "like an old sail endowed with life," — one of the Pilgrims, perhaps, who had "kept on the back side of the Cape and let the centuries go by;" or the free-spoken Wellfleet oysterman, "a poor good-for-nothing crittur," now "under petticoat government," who yet remembered

George Washington as a r-a-ther large and portly-looking man, with a pretty good leg as he sat on his horse;" or the iron-jawed Nauset woman, who seemed to be shouting at you through a breaker, and who looked "as if it made her head ache to live;" or the country soldier boy on his way to muster, in full regimentals, with shouldered musket and military step, who in a lonely place in the woods is suddenly abashed at the sight of a stranger approaching, and finds himself hard put to it to get by in anything like military order.

With men like these, natural men, Thoreau found himself at home; he described them almost as sympathetically as if they had been so many woodchucks or hen-hawks. As he said of his own boyhood, they were "part and parcel of nature" itself. As for fine manners parading about in fine clothes, how should he, a rustic jealous of his rusticity, presume to know what, if anything, might be going on under all that broadcloth? Reality was the chief of his ideals. The shabbiest of it was more to the purpose than a masquerade.

Whether it would have been better for

him had his taste been more liberal in this respect is a question about which it might be useless to speculate. Breadth may easily be sought at too great an expense, especially by one who has a distinct and highly individual work to accomplish. First of all, such a man must be himself. His imperfections, even, must be of his own kind, twin-born with his better qualities, a certain lack of complaisance being one of the likeliest and, in the strict sense, most appropriate. But that some of Thoreau's private and hasty remarks, in his letters and journals, about the meanness of his fellow-creatures, the more "respectable" among them, especially, might profitably have been left unprinted, is less open to doubt. They were expressions of moods rather than of convictions, it is fair to assume, and in any event would never have been printed by their author, one of whose cravings was for some kind of india-rubber that would rub out at once all which it cost him so many perusals and so much reluctance to erase. It is pretty hard justice that holds a man publicly to everything he scribbles in private,

— as if no allowance were to be made for whim and the provocation of the moment. The charm of a journal, as Thoreau says, consists in a "certain greenness." It is "a record of experiences and growth, not a preserve of things well done or said." After which it may be confessed that even from "Walden" and the "Week," published in the author's lifetime, it is possible to discover that charity and sweetness were not among his most distinguishing characteristics. Taste him after Gilbert White, and contrast the mellowness of the one with the sharp, assertive, acidulous quality of the other. Thoreau was a wild apple, and would have been proud of the name, suggestive of that "tang and smack" which he so feelingly celebrated. "Nonesuches" and "seek-no-furthers" were very tame and forgettable, he thought, as compared with the wildings, even the acrid and the puckery among which he begrudged to the cider-mill. It is in part this very "tang and smack," we may be sure, that makes his books keep so well in Time's literary cellar.

His humor, especially, "indispensable

pledge of sanity," as he calls it, is of that best of fruity flavors, a pleasant sour. Some, indeed, emulating his own fertility in paradox, have maintained that he had no humor, while others have rebuked him for priggishly excluding it from his later work. Did such critics never read "Cape Cod"? There, surely, Thoreau gave his natural drollery full play, — an almost antinomian liberty, to take a word out of those ecclesiastical histories, with the reading of which, under his umbrella, he so patiently enlivened his sandy march from Orleans to Provincetown. "As I sat on a hill one sultry Sunday afternoon," he says, "the meeting-house windows being open, my meditations were interrupted by the noise of a preacher who shouted like a boatswain, profaning the quiet atmosphere, and who, I fancied, must have taken off his coat. Few things could have been more disgusting or disheartening. I wished the tithing-man would stop him." Charles Lamb himself could hardly have bettered the delicious, biting absurdity of that final touch. It was not this Boanergian minister, but a man of an earlier generation, of whom we are told that he wrote a "Body of Divinity," "a book frequently sneered at, particularly by those who have read it."

The whole Cape, past and present, was looked at half quizzically by its inland visitor. The very houses "seemed, like mariners ashore, to have sat right down to enjoy the firmness of the land, without studying their postures or habiliments," — a description not to be fully appreciated except by those who have seen a Cape Cod village, with its buildings dropped here and there at haphazard upon the sand. Here, as everywhere, he was hungry for particulars; now improvising a rude quadrant with which to calculate the height of the bank at Highland Light, now, by ingenious but "not impertinent" questions, and for his private satisfaction only, getting at the contents of a schoolboy's dinner-pail, — the homeliest facts being always "the most acceptable to an inquiring mind." Thoreau's mother, by-the-bye, had some reputation as a gossip.

His work, humorous or serious, transcendental or matter-of-fact, is all the fruit of his own tree. Whatever its theme, nature or man, it is all of one spirit. Think what you will of it, it is never insipid. As his friend Channing said, it has its "stoical merits," its "uncomfortableness." Well might its author express his sympathy with the barberry bush, whose business is to ripen its fruit, not to sweeten it, — and to protect it with thorns. "Seek the lotus, and take a draught of rapture," was Margaret Fuller's rather high-flown advice to him; yet she too perceived that his mind was "not a soil for the citron and the rose, but for the whortleberry, the pine, or the heather." In all his books it would be next to impossible to find a pretty phrase or a sentimental one. He resorted to nature — in his less inquisitive hours — for the mood into which it put him, the invigoration, the serenity, the mental activity it communicated. But his pleasure in it, as compared with Wordsworth's or Hazlitt's, to take very dissimilar examples, was mostly an intellectual affair, the reader is tempted to say, though the remark needs qualification. One remembers such a passage as that descriptive of a winter twilight in Yellow Birch Swamp, where the gleams of the birches, as he came to one after another of them, "each time made his heart beat faster." Yet even here we are told of his ecstasy rather than made to feel it; and in general, surely, though he valued his emotions, and went to the woods and fields to enjoy them, they were such emotions as belonged to a pretty stoical sort of Epicurean; less rapturous than Wordsworth's, less tender than Hazlitt's, and with no trace of the brooding melancholy which makes the charm of books like Obermann and the journal of Amiel. He delighted in artless country music (it does not appear that he ever heard any other, and of course he felicitated himself upon this as upon all the rest of his poverty; it was only the depraved ear, he thought, that needed the opera), but let any reader try to imagine him writing this bit out of one of Hazlitt's essays:—

"I remember once strolling along the margin of a stream, skirted with willows and plashy sedges, in one of those low, sheltered valleys on Salisbury Plain, where the monks of former ages had planted chapels and built hermits' cells. There was a little parish church near, but tall elms and quivering alders hid it from sight, when, all of a sudden, I was startled by the sound of the full organ pealing on the ear, accompanied by rustic voices and the willing quire of village maids and children. It rose, indeed, 'like an exhalation of rich distilled perfumes.' The dew from a thousand pastures was gathered in its softness; the silence of a thousand years spoke in it. It came upon the heart like the calm beauty of death; fancy caught the sound, and faith mounted on it to the skies. It filled the valley like a mist, and still poured out its endless chant, and still it swells upon the ear, and wraps me in a golden trance, drowning the noisy tumult of the world!"

Here is another spirit than Thoreau's, another voice, another kind of prose — prose with the throb and even the accent of poetry. Stoics and spiritual economists do not write in this strain, nor is this the manner of a too envious observer of particulars. For better or worse, the prose of our poet-naturalist went squarely on its feet. His fancy might be never so nimble;

conceit and paradox might fairly make a cloud about him; but he essayed no flights. If his heart beat faster at some beauty of sight or sound, he said so quietly, with no change of voice, and passed on. As far as the mere writing went, it was done in straightforward, honest fashion, as if a man rather than an author held the pen.

Thoreau believed in well-packed sentences, each carrying its own weight, expressive of its own thought, rememberable and quotable. Of the beauties of a flowing style he had heard something too much. In practice, nevertheless, whether through design or by some natural felicity, he steered a middle course. The sentences might be complete in themselves, detachable, able to stand alone, but the paragraph never lacked a logical and even a formal cohesion. It was not a collection of "infinitely repellent particles," nor even a "basket of nuts." A great share of the writer's art, as he taught it, lay in leaving out the unessential, — the getting in of the essential having first been taken for granted. As for readers, in his more exalted moods he wished to write so well that there would be few to appreciate him; sometimes, indeed, he seemed to desire no readers at all. He speaks with stern disapproval of such as trouble themselves upon that point, and "would fain have one reader before they die." A lamentable weakness, truly.

In his present estate, however, let us hope that he carries himself a shade less haughtily, and is not above an innocent pleasure in the spread of his earthly fame, in new readers and new editions, and such choicely limited popularity as befits a classic. Even in his lifetime, as Emerson tells the story, he once tried to believe that something in his lecture might interest a little girl who told him she was going to hear it if it wasn't to be one of those old philosophical things that she didn't care about; and this although he had just been maintaining, characteristically, that whatever succeeded with an audience must be bad. He speaks somewhere against luxurious books, with superfluous paper and marginal embellishments. His taste was Spartan in those days. But he was never a stickler for consistency, and we may indulge a comfortable assurance that he takes no offense now at the sight of his Cape Cod journey — in which he worked so hard on that soft, leg-tiring Back-Side beach to get the ocean into him — decked out in colors and set forth sumptuously in two volumes. It is a very modest author who fears that his text will be outshone by any pictures, no matter how splendid. But who would have thought it, fifty years ago, — a book by the hermit of Walden in an *édition de luxe*, to lie on parlor tables! If only his father and his brother John could have seen it!

Thoreau believed in himself and in the soundness of his work. He coveted readers, and believed that he should have them. Without question he wrote for the future, and foresaw himself safe from oblivion. Emerson regretted Henry's want of ambition, we are told. He might have spared himself. "Show me a man who consults his genius," said Thoreau, "and you have shown me a man who cannot be advised." And he was the man. He was following an ambition of his own. If he did not keep step with his companions, it was because he "heard a different drummer." His ambition, and what seemed his wayward singularity, have been justified by the event. His "strange, self-centred, solitary figure, unique in the annals of literature," is in no danger of being forgotten. But what is most cheering about his present increasing vogue, especially in England, is that it arises from the very quality that Thoreau himself most prized, the innermost thing in him, — the loftiness and purity of his thought. Simplicity, faith, devotion to the essential and the permanent, — these were never more needed than now. These he taught, and, by a happy fate, he linked them with those natural themes that change not with time, and so can never become obsolete.

THOREAU'S DEMAND UPON NATURE

THOREAU'S DEMAND UPON NATURE

"I WISH to speak a word for Nature, for absolute freedom and wildness." So Thoreau began an article in "The Atlantic Monthly" forty-four years ago. He wished to make an extreme statement, he declared, in hope of making an emphatic one. Like idealists in general, — like Jesus in particular, — he believed in omitting qualifications and exceptions. Those were matters certain to be sufficiently insisted upon by the orthodox and the conservative, the minister and the school committee.

In an attempt at an extreme statement, Thoreau was very unlikely to fail. Thanks to an inherited aptitude and years of practice, there have been few to excel him with the high lights. In his hands exaggeration becomes one of the fine arts. We will not call it the finest art; his own best work would teach us better than that; but such as it is, with him to hold the brush, it would be difficult to imagine anything more effective. When he praises a quaking swamp as the most desirable of dooryards, or has visions of a people so enlightened as to burn all their fences and leave all the forests to grow, who shall contend with him? And yet the sympathetic reader — the only reader — knows what is meant, and what is not meant, and finds it good; as he finds it good when he is bidden to resist not a thief, or to hate his father and mother.

Thoreau's love for the wild — not to be confounded with a liking for natural history or an appreciation of scenery — was as natural and unaffected as a child's love of sweets. It belonged to no one part of his life. It finds utterance in all his books, but is best expressed, most feelingly and simply, and therefore most convincingly, in his journal, especially in such an entry as that of January 7, 1857, a bitterly cold, windy day, with snow blowing, — one of the days when "all animate things are reduced to their lowest terms." Thoreau has been out, nevertheless, for his afternoon walk, "through the woods toward the cliffs along the side of the Well Meadow field." Contact with Nature, even in this her severest mood, has given a quickening yet restraining grace to his pen. Now, there is no question of "emphasis," no plotting for an "extreme statement," no thought of dull readers, for whom the truth must be shown large, as it were, by some magic-lantern process. How differently he speaks! "Might I aspire to praise the moderate nymph Nature," he says, "I must be like her, moderate."

The passage is too long for quotation in full. "There is nothing so sanative, so poetic," he writes, "as a walk in the woods and fields even now, when I meet none abroad for pleasure. Nothing so inspires me, and excites such serene and profitable thought. . . . Alone in distant woods or fields, in unpretending sproutlands or pastures tracked by rabbits, even in a bleak and, to most, cheerless day like this, when a villager would be thinking of his inn, I come to myself, I once more feel myself grandly related. This cold and solitude are friends of mine. . . . I get away a mile or two from the town, into the stillness and solitude of nature, with rocks, trees, weeds, snow about me. I enter some glade in the woods, perchance, where a few weeds and dry leaves alone lift themselves above the surface of the snow, and it is as if I had come to an open window. I see out and around myself. . . . This stillness, solitude, wildness of nature is a kind of thoroughwort or boneset to my intellect. This is what I go out to seek. It is as if I always met in those places some grand, serene, immortal, infinitely encouraging, though invisible companion, and walked with him."

Four days later, dwelling still upon his "success in solitary and distant woodland walking outside the town," he says: "I do not go there to get my dinner, but to get that sustenance which dinners only preserve me to enjoy, without which dinners are a vain repetition. . . . I never chanced to meet with any man so cheering and elevating and encouraging, so infinitely suggestive, as the stillness and solitude of the Well Meadow field."

Language like this, though all may perceive the beauty and feel the sincerity of it, is to be understood only by those who are of the speaker's kin. It describes a country which no man knows unless he has been there. It expresses life, not theory, and calls for life on the part of the hearer.

And if the appeal be made to this tribunal, the language used here and so often elsewhere, by Thoreau, touching the relative inferiority of human society will neither give offense nor seem in any wise extravagant or morbid. Thoreau knew Emerson; he had lived in the same house with him; but even Emerson's companionship was less stimulating to him than Nature's own. Well, and how is it with ourselves, who have the best of Emerson in his books? Much as these may have done for us, have we never had seasons of communion with the life of the universe itself when even Emerson's words would have seemed an intrusion? Is not the voice of the world, when we can hear it, better than the voice of any man interpreting the world? Is it not better to hear for ourselves than to be told what another has heard? When the forest speaks things ineffable, and the soul hears what even to itself it can never utter, — for such an hour there is no book, there never will be. And if we wish not a book, no more do we wish the author of a book. We are in better company. In such hours, — too few, alas! — though we be the plainest of plain people, our own emotions are of more value than any talk. We know, in our measure, what Thoreau —

"An early unconverted Saint" —

was seeking words for when he said, "I feel my Maker blessing me."

To him, as to many another man, visitations of this kind came oftenest in wild and solitary places. Small wonder, then, that he loved to go thither. Small wonder that he found the pleasures of society unsatisfying in the comparison. There he communed, not with himself nor with his fellow, but with the "Wisdom and Spirit of the Universe." And when it is objected that this ought not to have been true, that he ought to have found the presence of men more elevating and stimulating than the presence of "inanimate" nature, we must take the liberty to believe that the critic speaks of that whereof he knows nothing. To revert to our own figure, he has never lived in Thoreau's country.

Thoreau was wedded to Nature not so much for her beauty as for delight in her high companionableness. There was more of Wordsworth than of Keats or Ruskin in him. He was more philosopher than poet, perhaps we may say. He loved spirit rather than form and color, though for these also his eye was better than most. Being a stoic, a born economist, a child of the pinched and frozen North, he felt most at home with Nature in her dull seasons. His delight in a wintry day was typical. He loved his mistress best when she was most like himself; as he said of human friendships, "I love that one with whom I sympathize, be she 'beautiful' or otherwise, of excellent mind or not." The swamp, the desert, the wilderness, these he especially celebrated. He began by thinking that nothing could be too wild for him; and even in his later years, notably in the "Atlantic" essay above quoted, he sometimes blew the same heroic strain. By this time, however, he knew and confessed, to himself at least, that there was another side to the story; that there was a dreariness beyond even his ready appreciation. More than once we find in his diary expressions like this, in late November: "Now a man will eat his heart, if ever, now while the earth is bare, barren, and cheerless, and we have the coldness of winter without the variety of ice and snow."

And what was true of seasons was, in the long run, equally true of places. Let them be wild, by all means, yet not too wild. When he returned from the Maine woods, he had seen, for the time being, enough of the wilderness. It was a relief to get back to the smooth but still varied landscape of eastern Massachusetts. That, for a permanent residence, seemed to him incomparably better than an unbroken forest. The poet must live open to the sky and the wind; his road must be prepared for him; and yet, "not only for strength, but for beauty, the poet must, from time to time, travel the logger's path and the Indian's trail, to drink at some new and more bracing fountain of the Muses." In short, the poet should live in Concord, and only once in a while seek the inspirations of the outer wilderness.

What we have called Thoreau's stoicism (knowing very well that he was not a stoic, except in some partial, looser meaning of the word), his liking for plainness and low expense, is perhaps at the base of one of his rarest excellencies as a writer upon nature, — his reserve and moderation. In statement, it is true, he could extravagate like a master. He boasts, as well he may, of his prowess in that direction; but in tone and sentiment, when it came to dealing, not with ethics or philosophy, but with the mistress of his affections, he kept always decently within bounds. He had a very sprightly fancy, when he chose to give it play; but he had with it, and controlling it, a prevailing sobriety, the tempering grace of good sense. "The alder," he says, "is one of the prettiest trees and shrubs in the winter. It is evidently so full of life, with its conspicuously pretty red catkins dangling from it on all sides. It seems to dread the winter less than other plants. It has a certain heyday and cheery look, less stiff than most, with more of the flexible grace of summer. With those dangling clusters of red catkins which it switches in the face of winter, it brags for all vegetation. It is not daunted by the cold, but still hangs gracefully over the frozen stream."

Most admirable, thrown in thus by the way, amid unaffected, matter-of-fact description and every-day sense, and with its homely "brags" and "switches" to hold it true, — to save it from a touch of foppery, a shade too much of prettiness. How differently some writers have dealt with similar themes: men so afraid of the commonplace as to be incapable of saying a thing in so many words, though it were only to mention the day of the week; men whose every other sentence must contain a "felicity;" whose pages are as full of floweriness and dainty conceits as a milliner's window; who surfeit you with confections, till you think of bread and water as a feast. Whether Thoreau's temperance is to be credited to the restraints of stoical philosophy or to plain good taste, it is a virtue to be thankful for.

With him the study of nature was not an amusement, nor even a more or less serious occupation for leisure hours, but the work of his life; a work to which he gave himself from year's end to year's end, as faithfully and laboriously, and with as definite a purpose, — a crop as truly in his eye, — as any Concord farmer gave himself to his farm. He was no amateur, no dilettante, no conscious hobbyist, laughing between times at his own absorption. His sense of a mission was as unquestioning as Wordsworth's, though happily there went with it a sense of humor that preserved it in good measure from over-emphasis and damaging iteration.

In degree, if not in kind, this whole-hearted, lifelong devotion was something new. It was one of Thoreau's originalities. To what a pitch he carried it, how serious and all-controlling it was, the pages of his journal bear continual witness. His was a Puritan conscience. He could never do his work well enough. After a eulogy of winter buds, "impregnable, vivacious willow catkins, but half asleep along the twigs" (there, again, is fancy of an uncloying type), he breaks out: "How healthy and vivacious must he be who would treat of these things. You must love the crust of the earth on which you dwell more than the sweet crust of any bread or cake; you must be able to extract nutriment out of a sand heap." "Must" was a great word with Thoreau. In hard times, especially, he braced himself with it. "The winter, cold and bound out as it is, is thrown to us like a bone to a famishing dog, and we are expected to get the marrow out of it. While the milkmen in the outskirts are milking so many scores of cows before sunrise, these winter mornings, it is our task to milk the winter itself. It is true it is like a cow that is dry, and our fingers are numb, and there is none to wake us up. . . . But the winter was not given us for no purpose. We must thaw its cold with our genialness. We are tasked to find out and appropriate all the nutriment it yields. If it is a cold and hard season, its fruit no doubt is the more concentrated and nutty."

In these winter journalizings, we not only have example and proof of the earnestness with which Thoreau pursued his outdoor studies, but are shown their method and their sufficient object. He was to be a writer, and nature was to be his theme, or, more exactly, his medium of expression. He required, therefore, in the way of raw material, a considerable store of outward knowledge, — knowledge of the outside or aspect of things, — classified, for convenience, as botany, ornithology, entomology, and the like; but after this, and infinitely more than this, he needed a living, deepening intimacy with the life of the world itself. For observation of the ways of plants and animals, of the phases of earth and sky, he had endless patience and all necessary sharpness of sense; work of this kind was easy, — he could do it in some good degree to his satisfaction; the vexatious thing about it was that it readily became too absorbing; but his real work, his *hard* work, the work that was peculiarly his, that taxed his capacities to the full, and even so was never accomplished, this work was not an amassing of relative knowledge, an accumulation of facts, a familiarizing of himself with appearances, but a perfecting of sympathy, the organ or means of that absolute knowledge which alone he found indispensable, which alone he cared greatly to communicate. There, except at rare moments, he was to the last below his ideal. His "task" was never done. His union with nature was never complete.

The measure of this union was gauged, as we have seen already, by its spiritual and emotional effects, by the mental states it brought him into; as the religious mystic measures the success of his prayers. He walked in the old Carlisle road, as the saint goes to his knees, to "put off worldly thoughts." The words are his own. There, when the hour favored him, he "sauntered near to heaven's gate."

It must be only too evident that success of this transcendental quality is not to be counted upon as one counts upon finding specimens for a botanical box. There is no comparison between scientific pursuits, so called, and this kind of supernatural history. For this, as Thoreau says, "you must be in a different state from common." "If it were required to know the position of the fruit dots or the character of the indusium, nothing could be easier than to ascertain it; but if it is required that you be affected by ferns, that they amount to anything, signify anything, to you, that they be another sacred scripture and revelation to you, helping to redeem your life, this end is not so easily accomplished."

This, then, it was for which Thoreau was ever on the alert; this was the prize set before him; this he required of ferns and clouds, of birds and swamps and deserted roads, — that they should stir him inwardly, that they should do something to redeem his life, or, as he said elsewhere, to affect the quality of the day. For this he cultivated the "fellowship of the seasons," a fellowship on which no man ever made larger drafts. Even when nature seemed to be getting "thumbed like an old spelling-book," even in the month that tempted him sometimes to "eat his heart," he still "sat the bench with perfect contentment, unwilling to exchange the familiar vision that was to be unrolled for any treasure or heaven that could be imagined." A new November was a novelty more tempting than any voyage to Europe or even to another world. "Young men have not learned the phases of nature:" so he comforted himself, when the fervors and inspirations of youth seemed at times to be waning: "I would know when in the year to expect certain thoughts and moods, as the sportsman knows when to look for plover."

Here, as everywhere with Thoreau, nature, in his ultimate conception of it, was nothing of itself. Everything is for man. This belief underlies all his writing upon natural themes, and, as well, all his personal dealings with the natural world. His idlest wanderings, whether in the Maine forests or in Well Meadow field, were made serious by it. To judge him by his own testimony, he seems to have known comparatively little of a careless, purposeless, childish delight in nature for its own sake. Nature was a better kind of book; and books were for improvement. In this respect he was sophisticated from his youth, like some model of "early piety." Nature was not his playground, but his study, his

Bible, his closet, his means of grace. As we have said, and as Channing long ago implied, his was a Puritan conscience. He must get at the heart of things, sparing no pains nor time, holding through thick and thin to the devotee's faith: "To him that knocketh it shall be opened." In this spirit he waited upon nature and the motions of his own genius. Patience, solitude, stillness, sincerity, and a quiet mind, — these were the instruments of his art. With them, not with prying sharp-sightedness, was the secret to be won. In his own phrase, characteristic in its homely expressiveness, if you would appreciate a phenomenon, though it be only a fern, you must "camp down beside it." And you must invent no distinctions of great and small. The humming of a gnat must be as significant as the music of the spheres.

Was he too serious for his own good, whether as man or as writer? And did he sometimes feel himself so? Was he whipping his own fault when he spoke against conscientious, duty-ridden people, and praised

"simple laboring folk
Who love their work,
Whose virtue is a song"?

It is not impossible, of course. But he, too, loved his work, — loved it so well as perhaps to need no playtime. Some have said that he made too much of his "thoughts and moods," that he was unwholesomely beset with the idea of self-improvement. Others have thought that he would have written better books had he stuck closer to science, and paid less court to poetry and Buddhistic philosophy. Such objections and speculations are futile. He did his work, and with it enriched the world. In the strictest sense it was his *own* work. If his ideal escaped him, he did better than most in that he still pursued it.

ROBERT LOUIS STEVENSON

ROBERT LOUIS STEVENSON

STEVENSON was one of the happy few: he knew his life's business from childhood. He was to write books. Happier still, and one of even a smaller minority, he early discovered that authorship is an art requiring a long and rigorous apprenticeship; that, if a man is to write, he must first study how, putting himself under tuition and devoting himself to practice; that an author no more than a pianist can begin with "pieces" and a public performance. In short, Stevenson had from the beginning an idea of literary composition as a fine art, — an art not to be picked up some pleasant day by the roadside (as later in life he essayed, for whim's sake, to pick up the art of writing music), nor carried away, as a matter of course, along with other more or less useful odds and ends of knowledge, from the grammar school or university, but to be acquired, if at all, by years on years of drill. Another man may write "well enough," and perhaps successfully, so far as material rewards go, by nature and the rule of thumb; but the artist aims at perfection, — perfection for its own sake. That aim, the pursuit of that ideal, is what *makes* him an artist. And such was Stevenson.

"All through my boyhood and youth," he says, "I was known and pointed out for the pattern of an idler; and yet I was always busy on my own private end, which was to learn to write. I kept always two books in my pocket, one to read, one to write in. As I walked, my mind was busy fitting what I saw with appropriate words; when I sat by the roadside, I would either read, or a pencil and a penny-version book would be in my hand, to note down the features of the scene or commemorate some halting stanzas."

So he "lived with words." And the point of the confession is that these "childish tasks," as he calls them in another place, were done "consciously for practice." "I had vowed that I would learn to write. That was a proficiency that tempted me; and I practiced to acquire it, as men learn to whittle, in a wager with myself."

But he did more than to practice. A man does not learn to whittle, or to paint, or to play the flute, by the primitive process of merely trying his hand, be it ever so patiently. The fine arts are no longer things to be invented, every man for himself. Others have whittled and painted; one generation has bequeathed its increment of skill to the next; here and there a master has arisen, and the masters have set up a standard; and now, the standard being established, the essential matter is, not to paint or write to the satisfaction of village critics, but to prove one's self a workman beside the best of the craft. For this there needs acquaintance with the masters' work, — such acquaintance, or so young Stevenson was persuaded, as could come from nothing but an imitative study of it. And he set himself to imitate. He had never heard the dictum, or he disbelieved it, that a boy should read the best writers, but pattern after nobody. Wherever he saw excellence of a kind that appealed to him, he took it for the time being as his model, a mark to aim at. This he did consciously and unashamed.

Such a course would never give him originality; but no matter. For the present it was not originality he was seeking; he was not yet writing books: he was learning his trade. Whether, having learned it, he should turn out to have original genius to go with his knowledge and put it to use, was a question that the event alone could determine. Originality is a gift of the gods; it is born with a man, or it is not born with him. The technique of a prose style, on the other hand, could be learned, and Stevenson's present business was to learn it, in the only way of which he had any knowledge, the way in which his masters themselves had learned it, — practice based on imitation.[1]

How could the boy have done better? He was called to write; he had "the love of words" which, as he says, marks the

[1] After he began writing, the question of an individual style took on, as was inevitable, a different complexion. In his early days he would not read Carlyle, and (more surprising) at forty or thereabout he discontinued the reading of Livy; dreading in both cases an injury to his own manner.

writer's vocation; and for such a boy "to work grossly at the trade, to forget sentiment, to think of his material and nothing else, is, for a while at least, the king's highway of progress." Yes, "for a while;" and after the while, if he is not merely one of the many that are called, but one of the few that are chosen, he will have found his own line, and such originality as nature endowed him with at birth (or before) will declare itself in the way appointed.

Stevenson had the name of an idler, he tells us, and it must be said that he wore it jauntily, — as he wore his old clothes. Whatever he did or failed to do, it would have been hard to catch him without defense. He wrote "An Apology for Idlers," which, as he confided to a correspondent, was "an apology for R. L. S.;" and to this day it sounds like a good one. It would do many a hard-working man and useful member of society a service to read it. He believed that, for the young especially, a certain kind and measure of idleness is a profitable kind of industry; while they are seemingly unemployed they may perchance be learning something that is really worth while: "to play the fiddle, to know a good cigar, or to speak with ease and opportunity to all varieties of men."

For himself, like many another man of genius, he was very little of a scholar in the traditional sense of the word. What the schools had taken upon themselves to teach were mostly not the things that he had taken upon himself to learn. At the university he devised "an extensive and highly rational system of truantry," and no one "ever had more certificates (of attendance) for less education." Like his antitype in Mr. Barrie's novel, he could always find a way. No doubt his personal attractiveness counted for much here, as it did everywhere. One of his earlier teachers had pronounced him "without exception the most delightful boy he ever knew;" and his mother's testimony is that his masters found it pleasanter to talk with him than to teach him. How his wits and his fine gift of plausibility helped him over a hard place in one of the last of his examinations — for admission to the bar — is related as from himself, by Mr. Balfour.[*] The subject in hand was "Ethical and Metaphysical Philosophy," and a certain book had been prescribed. "The examiner asked me a question," Stevenson says, "and I had to say to him, 'I beg your pardon, but I do not understand your phraseology.' 'It's the text-book,' he said. 'Yes; but you could n't possibly expect me to read so poor a book as that.' He laughed like a hunchback, and then put the question in another form. I had been reading Mayne, and answered him by the historical method. They were probably the most curious answers ever given in the subject. I don't know what he thought of them, but they got me through."

It is a good story, and thoroughly characteristic. There was nothing academic in Stevenson's turn of mind, whether in youth or manhood. "I was inclined to regard any professor as a joke," he remarks, in his "Memoir of Fleeming Jenkin," and the words may be taken as fairly expressive of his attitude toward the whole business of what is called education. The last thing he meant to be was a conventional man, — "a consistent first-class passenger in life," — and why should he disquiet himself over a conventional training? Allow him his own subject and his own method, and he would be studious with anybody.

So throughout his early years, as we have seen, he studied the art of authorship. Then, as happens to all artists, came the critical point of production or nonproduction: Would the plant so sedulously watered and tended, so promising in the leaf, prove to be fertile or sterile? Having so lofty an idea of his art, so exalted a standard of excellence in it, would he go on indefinitely putting himself off with preparations, "prelusory gymnastic," as he saw so many painters doing at Barbizon ("snoozers" instead of painters, covering their walls with studies, and never coming to the picture), and as is so easy for art students of all kinds to do, or, having learned the handling of his tools, would he set himself to use them in the performance of a man's work?

Such a question is by no means one that answers itself. In any particular case there is perhaps more than an even chance that the student will never have the industry, the courage, and the intellectual and moral stuff to accomplish, or even seriously put his hand to, any of the great things for which he has so long been making ready. Stevenson himself, from all that appears, may have had at the beginning a period when the issue hung more or less in doubt. "I remember a time," he wrote afterward, "when I was very idle, and lived and profited by that humor." Now, he says, the case is different with him, he knows not why. Perhaps it is "a change of age." He made many slight efforts at reform, "had a thousand skirmishes to keep himself at work upon particular mornings;" the life of Goethe affected him, as did also some noble remarks of Balzac, but he was never conscious of a struggle, "never registered a vow, nor seemingly had anything personally to do with the matter." "I came about like a well-handled ship," he concludes. "There stood at the wheel that unknown steersman whom we call God."

In his twenty-fourth or twenty-fifth year, at all events, he was really getting under way, though for the present, as was becoming, with small ventures; and from that time, except for the frequent occasions when illness and the likelihood of speedy death constrained him to "twiddle his fingers and play patience," he kept his pen busy as few men of anything like his physical disabilities and his roving disposition have ever done. For it is important to note that he was by inheritance a wanderer. Even had his health allowed it, he could never have sat month after month at the same ·desk, turning off so many hundred words as his daily stint. Once, when he has lived for six months at Davos, he writes to his friend Colvin that he is in a bad way, — a result, he believes, of having been too long in one place. "That tells on my old gypsy nature; like a violin hung up, I begin to lose what music there was in me." And when his mother complained that he was little at home, he bade her not be vexed at his nomadic habits. "I *must* be a bit of a vagabond; it's your own fault, after all, is n't it? You should n't have had a tramp for a son."

For a man who had studied authorship, and wished to write not mainly from books, but from the experience of his own mind and body, this ineradicable gypsy strain was of the highest value. How much it imported to Stevenson should be evident even to those who know his books only by the backs of them. Bodily health excepted, he had all the qualifications of a traveler. Happy man that he was, he was always a boy, rich to the last in some of the best of youthful virtues, — buoyancy, curiosity, "interest in the whole page of experience," and the capacity for surprise. The world for him was never an old story. When he saw a ship or a train of cars, he wished himself aboard. Discomforts and dangers were nothing; nay, they could be turned into excellent fun, and after that into almost as excellent copy. His spirit was habitually strung up to out-of-door pitch, to borrow his own expression. He felt "the incommunicable thrill of things." Not for him a staid life in drawing-rooms or city clubs. He would be out in the open, "where men still live a man's life." At forty he wrote his own formula thus: "0.55 artist, 0.45 adventurer." Near the same time, being just from the island of Molokai, where he had played croquet with seven leper girls (and would not wear gloves, though cautioned to that effect, lest it should make the girls unhappy to be reminded of their condition), he writes to a friend: "This climate; these voyagings; these landfalls at dawn; new islands peaking from the morning bank; new forested harbors; new passing alarms of squalls and surf; new interests of gentle natives, — the whole tale of my life is better to me than any poem." A lucky combination it was, both for the man himself and for the world of readers, — fifty-five per cent artist, and forty-five per cent adventurer.

And the adventures, of course, need not be so extraordinarily venturesome, with an artist's pen to put them on the paper. In 1887 Stevenson had been once more at the gates of death with hemorrhages, this time so often repeated that they had ceased almost to be exciting, and were rather grown tiresome; and when the doctors prescribed another change of climate, he sailed for America. The steamer turned out to be loaded with cattle, — "a ship with no style on, and plenty of sailors to talk to;"

and this is how the consumptive patient describes the voyage: "I was so happy on board that ship, I could not have believed it possible. We had the beastliest weather, and many discomforts; but the mere fact of its being a tramp-ship gave us many comforts; we could cut about with the men and officers, stay in the wheel-house, discuss all manner of things, and really be a little at sea. . . . My heart literally sang. . . . It is worth having lived these last years, partly because I have written some better books, which is always pleasant, but chiefly to have had the joy of this voyage."

Later, in the South Seas, he ran more than once upon the very edge of shipwreck, but always with the same brave heart and the same gayety. "We had a near squeak," he writes to a friend, after one such experience. "The reefs were close in with, my eye! what a surf! The pilot thought we were gone, and the captain had a boat cleared, when a lucky squall came to our rescue. My wife, hearing the order given about the boats, remarked to my mother, 'Is n't that nice? We shall soon be ashore!' Thus does the female mind unconsciously skirt along the verge of eternity." And thus, be it added, does the artistic masculine mind turn even the face of death itself "to favor and to prettiness."

By this time Stevenson had almost settled it with himself that he should never again leave the sea. "My poor grandfather, it is from him that I inherit the taste, I fancy, and he was round many islands in his day; but I, please God, shall beat him at that before the recall is sounded. . . . Life is far better fun than people dream who fall asleep among the chimney-stacks and telegraph wires." One feels like saying again, What a blessing it was for the world that a man so perennially boyish, so endowed with the capacity for enjoyment, so conscious of his life, so incurably in love with the romantic side of things, was also the master of a style and an industrious lover of the art of writing!

His remark, quoted above, about the "plenty of sailors to talk to" suggests another thing: his exceeding fondness for rubbing elbows with what are called, inappropriately enough, common people, — people who have lived free from the leveling, uniformity-producing, character-dulling, commonizing influences of too many books and an excess of social sophistication. This, too, was a real fairy's gift to a man destined for literature. "He was of a conversible temper" (he is speaking of himself in his youth), "and insatiably curious in the aspects of life." Like Will o' the Mill, "he had a taste for other people, and other people had a taste for him." As we read of his journeyings hither and thither, and the friends he made almost as often as he opened his mouth, we are reminded of what David Balfour's father said of his offspring: "He is a steady lad and a canny goer; and I doubt not he will come safe, and be well liked where he goes." Perhaps it was from his own experience that Stevenson was writing when he said that a boy might learn in his truant hours "to know a good cigar, or to speak with ease and opportunity to all varieties of men."

Stevenson's books, the narratives of travel and the essays not less than the novels, — perhaps even more, — are galleries of portraits. Wherever he went, he found men: not caricatures, mere burlesques and oddities, cheap material for print, creatures of a single crying peculiarity, so easily drawn and, for one reading, so "effective;" nor lay figures simply, wire frames (literature is populated with them) on which to hang "the trappings of composition;" but breathing men, full, like the rest of us, of complexity and paradox, nobly designed, perhaps, but — still like the rest of us — more or less spoiled in the making; men who had known, each for himself, the war in the members (happy for them if they knew it still!), and had drunk, every one, of the mingled cup of tragedy and comedy. He loved the sight of them; their talk, wise or foolish, was music to his ears; and the queerest and ugliest of them, under his capable and affectionate hand, wear something of a human grace upon the canvas.

It is a great gallery. Who that has ever walked there will forget the old soldier turned beggar, the borrower of poets' books? — "the wreck of an athletic man, tall, gaunt, and bronzed; far gone in consumption, with that disquieting smile of the mortally stricken in his face; but still active afoot, still with the brisk military carriage, the ready military salute." We can see him, "striding forward uphill, his staff now clapped to the ribs of his deep, resonant chest, now swinging in the air with the remembered jauntiness of the private soldier; and all the while his toes looking out of his boots, and his shirt looking out of his elbows, and death looking out of his smile, and his big, crazy frame shaken by accesses of cough." His honest head may have been "very nearly empty, his intellect like a child's," but he loved the unexpected words and the moving cadence of good verse. We know his talk; a little more, and we should hear it: "Keats, — John Keats, sir, — he was a very fine poet."

A book like "The Amateur Emigrant" is full of such sketches, every one done from life, and hit off with a perfection that might well render it and the volume, as foolish mortals say, "immortal." It would be long to enumerate them, though it is a short book. There is Jones the Welshman, for example, — "my excellent friend Mr. Jones," owner and dispenser of the Golden

Oil; "hovering round inventions like a bee over a flower, and living in a dream of patents." He had been rich, and now was poor, but, like all dabblers in patents, he had "a nature that looked forward." "If the sky were to fall to-morrow, I should look to see Jones, the day following, perched on a step-ladder and getting things to rights." What *we* should have cared most to see was Mr. Jones and Mr. Stevenson walking the deck by the hour and dissecting their neighbors; for Jones was first of all a student of character. "Whenever a quaint or human trait slipped out in conversation, you might have seen Jones and me exchanging glances; and we could hardly go to bed in comfort till we had exchanged notes and discussed the day's experience. We were then like a couple of anglers comparing a day's kill." And there is the fiddler, "carrying happiness about with him in his fiddle-case," a "white-faced Orpheus cheerily playing to an audience of white-faced women," with his fiery bit of a brother, who "made a god of the fiddler," and was determined that everybody else should do the same; and Mackay, the cynic and debater, who professed to believe in nothing but what had to do with food ("that's the bottom and the top"), but who once grew so eager in maintaining this noble thesis that he slipped the meal hour, and was compelled, with a smile of shamefacedness, to go without his tea; and Barney the Irishman, the universal favorite, so natural and happy, with his "tight little figure, unquenchable gayety, and indefatigable good will," who could sing most acceptably and play all manner of innocent pranks, but whose "drab clothes were immediately missing from the group" when, after the ladies had retired, some one struck up an indecent song; and the sick man (poor soul), who thought it was "by" with him, and who had a good house at home, and "no call to be here;" and the two stowaways, so fond of each other, yet so strikingly contrasted, — one so ready to work for his passage, the other "a skulker in the grain," and like the devil himself for lying.

And besides these there are numbers more nearly or quite as telling; but they must be let pass, though it is pleasant to pick good things out of a book that, comparatively speaking, seems to have been little made of, either by the author or by his admirers. To one of these, at least, "The Amateur Emigrant" seems, not one of Stevenson's greatest books, indeed, but certainly one of the most enjoyable, say on the sixth or eighth reading.

It is a point of grace with any writer, and a very *sine qua non* with the essayist, that he should be able to speak often of himself without offense, as Montaigne and Lamb did, to mention two shining and incontestable examples. And the trick (though it is not a trick, but an admirable quality, and almost as far as honesty from being common) is none of your easy ones. To begin with, the venturer on such an experiment must be interested in himself, which is by no means an ordinary happening. Most men, we may say, count for nullities under this head; they recognize their outward presentments in the glass, no doubt, and are letter-perfect with their names and occupations; but for a knowledge of their inner selves, the story of their real lives, the "wonderful pageant of consciousness," one might almost as well interrogate the lamp-post on the next corner. They have never kept company with their own thoughts, nor been in the least degree inquisitive about them. Life, as they live it, is a matter of externals, of eating and drinking and being clothed, of getting and spending more or less money, of being amused, of movings up or down on a social ladder. As for the past, the past of themselves, — which with another man is his dearest possession, — it is mainly as if it had never been. They must have had a boy's dreams once, one would think, but that was long, long ago, and the dreamer is dead, and his dreams with him.

But if a man is to tell the world about himself, and charm it into attention, he must not only be in love with his subject; he must have a natural frankness, an unaffected and almost unconscious delight in self-revelation, — tempered by a decent sense of personal privacy, — such as infallibly commends itself and makes its way, the listener cannot tell how. In other words, and in a good sense, the man must be still a boy, endowed with a boy's winning attributes, and entitled, therefore, to something of a boy's privilege. And with all the rest, and among the most important, he must be favored with the gracious quality of humor. Of all talk whatsoever, talk about one's self must not be too serious. No man (or none but a great poet) can safely indulge in it unless it is natural for him to see the funny side of his own foibles, and at the right minute to make his point at his own expense. All of which is perhaps no more than to say that the writer in the first person must be a man of taste, knowing (a wisdom which nobody under the sun can teach him) what to say and what not to say, and, chiefest of all, how and when to say it.

Stevenson did not talk of himself so freely as Montaigne (how could he, in these proper days?) nor, the present scribe being judge, so adorably as Lamb. Nature herself is little likely to hit the white centre of perfection twice, and we shall perhaps see another Shakespeare as soon as another Lamb; but few have loved a personal theme better, and in the handling of it there were none among the living to surpass him. He had every qualification for the work. A pity he died at forty-four,— a pity in every aspect of the case, but especially when it is considered what treasures of youthful reminiscence he would have left behind him had he lived even to the approaches of old age. Such a devotee of his own past should have been spared to see it through a bluer haze. Yet even in middle life how fair it looked to him, and how lovingly he laid its colors as he transferred the picture to the page! Hear him speak of his grandfather, in a passage no better than is common with him, and dealing with nothing out of the ordinary: —

"Now I often wonder what I have inherited from this old minister. I must suppose, indeed, that he was fond of preaching sermons, and so am I, though I never heard it maintained that either of us loved to hear them. He sought health in his youth in the Isle of Wight, and I have sought it in both hemispheres; but whereas he found and kept it, I am still on the quest. He was a great lover of Shakespeare, whom he read aloud, I have been told, with taste; well, I love my Shakespeare, also, and am persuaded I can read him well, though I own I never have been told so. He made embroidery, designing his own patterns; and in that kind of work I never made anything but a kettle-holder in Berlin wool, and an odd garter of knitting, which was as black as the chimney before I had done with it. He loved port, and nuts, and porter; and so do I, but they agreed better with my grandfather, which seems to me a breach of contract. He had chalkstones in his fingers; and these in good time I may inherit, but I would much rather have inherited his noble presence. Try as I please, I cannot join myself on with the reverend doctor; and all the while, no doubt, and even as I write the phrase, he moves in my blood, and whispers words to me, and sits efficient in the very knot and centre of my being."

A man could talk of himself in that strain till the sun put the stars out, and nobody would vote him tiresome or blame him for an egotist. Yes, a misfortune it was that he could not have lived to write a dozen books full of essays like "The Manse," "Old Mortality," "Memoirs of an Islet," and especially "A Gossip on a Novel of Dumas's." So appreciative a reader and so entertaining a talker could never have wearied us with gossip of his favorite books, "the inner circle of his intimates;" and the more first-personal and confidential he became, the better we should have liked it.

Well, since we cannot have the finished essays, we will be the more thankful for the letters. How good they are! — so varied, so spontaneous, so free-spoken, so humanly wise and so deliciously nonsensical; now bubbling over with jest, now touching the deepest springs of thought and action; fit expression of a man who was himself both Ariel and Prospero; "an old, stern, unhappy devil of a Norseman," yet with "always some childishness on hand;" the "grandson of the Manse," who would rise from the grave to preach, and has "scarce broken a commandment to mention," yet owning it as his darling wish to be a pirate. Whim and opinion, settled conviction and passing mood, alike find utterance in them; and best of all, perhaps, many of them are most engagingly rich in matter connected with his own pursuit. A selection of these in a handy volume (why must letters always be put up in a form too cumbersome for lovers' convenience, as if they, more than other books, were expected to stand forever upon a shelf?) would go far to supply the place of that treatise on "The Art of Literature" which their author spoke so frequently of making.

Here would be found a letter to Mr. Marcel Schwob, a letter one page long, but weighty with the subtlest and pithiest criticism, not of Mr. Schwob's writings alone (that might not seem so very important), but of writing in general, and in particular of Stevenson's. For it is impossible to read it without perceiving that the critic is passing judgment (no unkind one) upon his own early books of sentimental travel. His correspondent has sent him a volume of verses. He has read it through twice, and is reading it again, — a handsome compliment, to start with. It is essentially graceful, he says, but is a thing of promise rather than a thing final in itself. "You have yet to give to us — and I am expecting it with impatience — something of a larger gait; something daylit, not twilit; something with the colors of life, not the flat tints of a temple illumination; something that shall be *said* with all the clearnesses and the trivialities of speech, not *sung* like a semi-articulate lullaby. It will not please yourself as well, but it will please others better. It will be more of a whole, more worldly, more nourished, more commonplace — and not so pretty, perhaps not even so beautiful. No man knows better than I that, as we go on in life, we must part from prettiness and the graces. We but attain qualities to lose them; life is a series of farewells, even in art; even our proficiencies are deciduous and evanescent. So here with these exquisite pieces, . . . you will perhaps never excel them. . . . Well, you will do something else, and of that I am in expectation."

Happy poet! to be caressed so affectionately and lanced so beneficently with one stroke of the master's hand; and happy critic, no less! having sentences of this quality to drop without a second thought, like small change from the hand of wealth, into the oblivion of private correspondence.

In truth, Stevenson could afford to be generous; he had always good things enough and to spare. His was a mind incessantly active. He was always covering paper. If only disease would leave him strength enough to hold the pen, he could be trusted to keep it going. Ideas thronged upon him; books by the dozen, one may almost say, stood waiting for him to make them. The more wonder that, with all this excess of fertility, he could yet rewrite and rewrite, and then write again, still on the search for perfection. Surely the artist was strong in him.

His fame was of slow growth, surprising as the fact seems now, till he wrote novels. These, as all the world knows, since all the world reads them, are nothing like the ordinary modern novel of carpet knights and pairs of happy or unhappy lovers. They are romances in the heroic vein, spun mostly of a single thread, with no lack of high lights, plenty of blood-letting, a good spice of humor, dialogue that is closely pared and talks of itself, character displayed in action, not dissected, and movement to delight the lover of a story.

The lode was struck, almost by accident, when Stevenson's schoolboy stepson, backed by another "schoolboy in disguise," — namely, Stevenson's father, — begged him to "write something interesting." The response to this reasonable request was "Treasure Island," which not only filled the schoolboys' bill, but captivated so stout-hearted a disbeliever in things romantic as Mr. Henry James. As it was this story that introduced its author to a wider public, he used to speak of it (possibly with a shade of irony, though that does not certainly appear) as his first book.

It may be that the gift of romance was the highest of his endowments. Some, at least, have thought so, and have reckoned the novels as not only the most popular, but the greatest of his works. As to the choice among them, the question of their comparative excellence among themselves, that is a matter not under discussion here, the writer of the present paper having no sort of competency for dealing with it. His own special delight is in "David Balfour" (the two parts) and "Treasure Island." These he hopes to read — now and then a chapter, if no more — as long as he reads anything. He likes the men, — and the women, — and he likes the talk. Mr. James's comment upon "Treasure Island," that one seems to be reading it over a schoolboy's shoulder, strikes him as extremely ingenious and pretty, but he is conscious of nothing of that nature himself. He reads it, if he may be allowed to say so, on his own hook, and for the time being is himself the schoolboy, — which may or may not be the better fun. He likes the story and the pictures, — for every chapter *is* a picture, — and he likes the writing.

Concerning this last point, so often discussed, what shall be said? As Stevenson's nature was complex and his themes varied, so he wrote in many keys. His prose was never "far from variation and quick change." When he put pen to any work, — essay, travel, sketch, tragedy, or comedy, — the first thing was to strike "the essential note." He would not begin a funeral march in A major, nor a sailor's hornpipe in C minor; a requiem for the friend of his youth was one thing, and a description of his fellow passengers in the steerage was another: and, strange to tell, here and there a wise critic, wise above what is written, has discovered in this change of key proof of a want of originality. "Behold," he cries, "the man has no style of his own; to-day he writes in one manner, and to-morrow in another." The same sharp-eyed reviewers are certain to be troubled because Stevenson talks freely of style, openly professing to have cultivated one, — to have cared not only for what he said, but almost or quite as much for the way in which he said it. "How can a man be concerned with the niceties of expression, and yet be true to himself?" they seem ready to ask. A question to which, it must be admitted, there is no answer, or none worth the offering to any who need to ask for it.

To be greatly occupied with matters of form is doubtless to subject one's self to peril. Careful writing may easily become mannered (as careless writing also may, and with less excuse); but what then? Danger is the common lot. An author, not less than other men, must face it, whether he will or no. He may choose between one set of pitfalls and another, but he will find no path without them. As for the risk of mannerism, Stevenson escaped it substantially unharmed. Compared with some of the more famous of his style-loving contemporaries, he may be said to have come off without a scratch. Whether his style is better or worse than theirs (and touching a point so delicate an unprofessional critic may prudently reserve his opinion) is a different matter; at least, it is less tagged with peculiarity. It was formed, as style should be, by the study of many models, not of one; and it has many virtues, including in good measure one of the highest, rarest, and most elusive, the quality of pleasurableness, or charm, — a quality not to be acquired by labor, nor to be exactly defined; a something added to a thing already complete, like the bloom on the grape or the perfume of the rose.

If the style has failings, also; if one feels now and then, in the more closely wrought of the essays especially, a certain excess of precision, a seeming hardness of outline, a lack, shall we say, of flexibility; if, after a time, one experiences a sensation as of walking in too continuously strong a light, with the sun, as it were, standing still at high noon; if one misses those momentary glimpses of invisible truth, those hints and adumbrations of things beyond the writer's and the reader's ken (a feeling as if twilight were coming on, and shadows were falling across the page), those touches of distance and mystery which make the peculiar attractiveness of another order of writing; if this, and perhaps more than this (an occasional want of absolute success in the use of the file; a failure, that is to say, to leave the phrase looking only the more unstudied for the labor bestowed upon it), — if things like these are felt at times by the sensitive reader, what does it all signify but that, in the perception and expression of truth, as in the making of moral character, one excellence of necessity excludes or dwarfs another, and perfection is still to seek? As the French martyr said ("a dread confession," Stevenson called it, in one of his moods), "Prose is never done."

The estimate which the author himself placed upon his style (though this is a point of little consequence) seems not to have been exalted. He had his gift, he knew, and had done his best to improve it; but other men had greater ones. He was an enthusiastic reader, and while still fresh from the enjoyment of "A Window in Thrums," he wrote to Mr. Barrie: "There are two of us now [two Scotchmen] that the Shirra might have patted on the head. And please do not think, when I seem thus to bracket myself with you, that I am wholly blinded with vanity. Jess is beyond my frontier line; I could not touch her skirt; I have no such glamour of twilight on my pen. I am a capable artist; but it begins to look to me as if you were a man of genius. Take care of yourself for my sake."

A handsome thing for a man to write, and a pleasant thing for his lovers to remember, but, as we say, not to be interpreted too strictly, as if it settled anything. The more considerable a man's gifts, the more likely he is to speak disparagingly of them. To take his own word for it, Stevenson was a poor letter-writer, "essentially and originally incapable." So he assures one of his correspondents; and then, the mood coming on him, he proceeds to cover page after page with the very scintillations of epistolary genius, — compliment, gossip, humor, brilliant description, verbal felicities, sweetness of personal feeling, everything, in short, that goes to the making of a perfect letter. No doubt he smiled at the incongruity of the thing as he folded the sheet (for no doubt he knew he had done well), but what shall we conclude as to the value of an honest author's depreciatory judgment of his own work? If it is not a proverb, it ought to be, that self-dispraise goes little ways.

The welcome of Stevenson to his younger Scotch contemporary was characteristic of the man. In all his letters there is not a glimmer of professional jealousy nor a word of belittling criticism. With all his boyishness, — partly because of it, it might be truer to say, — he had a manly heart. Generosity and courage were matters of course with him, native to the blood. In his novels there is plenty — some would say a superfluity — of battle, murder, and sudden death; Cut and Thrust were two of his favorite heroes; he loved the breath of danger, and when, for the first and last time, he saw armed men taking the field, "the old aboriginal awoke" in him, and he sniffed the air like a war horse; he could be stern as the Judgment Day itself against injustice and cruelty; in such a cause he would break a lance, though all the world should call him, what he was once overheard to call himself, another Don Quixote; but withal, few men were ever more tender-hearted. At twenty-one, as he told the story more than twenty years afterward, he enjoyed a great day of fishing; the trout so many and so hungry that in his eagerness he forgot to kill them one by one as he took them from the water. In the small hours of the night his conscience smote him; he saw the fishes "still kicking in their agony;" and he never fished again. Whoever was in distress was sure not only of his sympathy, but of his hand and purse. He would walk the streets of a city half the night with a lost child in his arms, invalid though he was; and when he comes to clear the land of his new South Sea domain, he wonders whether any one else ever felt toward Nature just as he does. He pities the vines and grasses that he uproots: "their struggles go to my heart like supplications." Since his death, says his biographer, the native chiefs — "gentle barbarians," truly — have forbidden the use of firearms on the hillside where he is buried, "that the birds may live there undisturbed."

Stevenson believed in the supremacy of the soul. He would not be put down by things material. Many years he lived face to face with death, and to the last his testimony was that he found his life good. To a critic who thought him too little appreciative of the darker side of human existence he wrote: "If you have had trials, sickness, the approach of death, the alienation of friends, poverty at the heels, and have not felt your soul turn round upon these things and spurn them under, you must be very differently made from me, and, I earnestly believe, from the majority of men." Such was his brave confession; and his life, from all we see of it, was in full accordance with his faith. It might be said of him what Lowell said of Chaucer: he was "so truly pious that he could be happy in the best world that God chose to make."

Toward the last, it is true, he fell into a state of depression, and for a time was alarmingly unlike his old self. His power of work seemed to be gone, and the "complicated miseries" that surrounded him weighed hard upon his spirits. Even then, however, he protested his belief in "an ultimate decency of things; ay, and if I woke in hell, should still believe it." This was his natural religion, which the early loss of his ancestral creed — that "damnatory creed" with which his childhood was "pestered almost to madness" — had only deepened and irradiated. And the dark and sterile mood was no more than a mood, after all. Soon he was writing again, more successfully than ever. And then, with everything bright before him, his powers working at their easiest and best, his prayer for "courage, gayety, and the quiet mind" fully answered, all at once the end came. The brief candle, that so often had flickered and burned low, was suddenly blown out. He had gone round more islands than his lighthouse-building grandfather, as it amused him once to boast, and now, like his grandfather, he had reached "the end of all his cruising."

> "Home is the sailor, home from sea,
> And the hunter home from the hill."

Over his grave, almost before his body could be lowered into it, there rose the inevitable buzz of critical surmise and questioning. Human nature is impatient. It believes in ranks and orders, and must have the labels on at once. Were Stevenson's books really great, it desired to know, — as great as those of such and such another man? Or were his admirers — whose regrets and acclamations, it must be owned, made at that minute a pretty busy chorus — setting him on too lofty a pedestal and stirring about him too dense a "dust of praise"? A few disinterested souls seemed surely to believe it, and were in great perturbation accordingly. To listen to them one might have supposed that the very foundations were being destroyed. And then what should the righteous do?

They need not have troubled themselves. The world will last a long time yet, and our little breath of praise or blame will speedily blow itself out and be forgotten. As was said of Hazlitt, so it must be said of Stevenson: Time will tell. Not that it will of necessity tell the truth; since what we dignify as the verdict of Time is, after all, in a certain way of looking at it, nothing but the opinion of the majority; but at least it will have the force of a last word, — there will be nobody to dispute it.

Meanwhile, there is no reason in the nature of things why those who admire Stevenson, or any other contemporary, should be frightened out of saying so. Our judgment may be wrong, of course; but also it may be right; and right or wrong, if it be modestly held, there can be no law against its utterance. And if we are to speak at all, we must speak while we can, —unless, to be sure, we are to call no man happy till after *we* are dead.

A RELISH OF KEATS

A RELISH OF KEATS

In all the writing of genius, which is a power that possesses its so-called possessor rather than is possessed by him, there is much that seems like accident. Many things — all the best ones, it might not be too much to say — are contributed by the pen rather than by the man. The man had never thought of them; it was no more within his intention to write them than to write another "Hamlet;" and suddenly there they are before him on the paper. The handwriting is his, but as to where the words came from, he can tell hardly more than his most illiterate neighbor. From No-Man's-Land, if you please to say so.

Keats was proudly conscious of this mystery. There is nothing, indeed, upon which he, or any poet, could half so reasonably felicitate himself. His divinest verses, he knew it and owned it, were traced for him by "the magic hand of chance." A great thing, a power almost omnipotent, is this that we call by that convenient, ignorance-disguising name. It made not only Keats's verses, but Keats himself. Otherwise how explain him? — son of a stable-keeper, a play-loving, belligerent, unstudious boy, a surgeon's apprentice at fifteen, dead at twenty-six, and before that — and henceforth — one of the chief glories of England, a poet, "with Shakespeare."

He himself suspected nothing of his gift, so far as appears, till he was eighteen. Then he read the "Fairy Queen," fell under its enchantment, and immediately, or very soon, minding an inward call, began trying his own hand at verses. At first they were no more than verses, "neither precocious nor particularly promising," says Mr. Colvin; things that a man takes a certain pleasure in doing, —

> "There is a pleasure in poetic pains
> Which only poets know," —

and finds, it may be, a certain kind of profit in doing, but sees to be of no value as soon as they are done.

At twenty the vein began to show the gold. He assayed the shining particles, for by this time he had been reading Shakespeare and Milton, and knew a line of poetry when he saw it,[1] and, like the man in the parable, he did not hesitate. He knew what he wanted. He would sell all that he had and buy that field. "I begin," he said, in one of the earliest of his extant letters, — "I begin to fix my eye upon one horizon." He would be a poet, because he must. He would not be a surgeon, because he must not. He had done well in his studies, we are told, and was in good repute at the hospital, whither by this time he had gone; but a voice was speaking within him, and there was never an hour but he heard it. "The other day, during the lecture," he said, "there came a sunbeam into the room, and with it a whole troop of creatures floating in the ray; and I was off with them to Oberon

---

[1] How largely he profited by his study of Spenser, Shakespeare, Milton, and other poets, especially in the enrichment of his vocabulary, is shown by Mr. E. de Sélincourt in the notes and appendices to his recent admirable edition of Keats's *Poems*. The subject is interesting, and is treated in the most painstaking manner.

and fairy-land." "My last operation," he tells another correspondent, "was the opening of a man's temporal artery. I did it with the utmost nicety, but reflecting on what passed through my mind at the time, my dexterity seemed a miracle, and I never took up the lancet again."

It was a bold stroke, — no prudent adviser would have borne him out in it, — to forsake everything else to be a poet. But never was a luckier one. He had but four or five years to live, and (a comfort indeed to think of!) he did not waste them in making ready to earn a living he was never to have. It was a plain case of losing one's life to find it.

Only four or five years, but with what a zest he lived them! Misgivings no doubt he had, enough and to spare. Now and then, to use his own words, he was pretty well "down in the mouth." "I have been in such a state of mind," he writes to Haydon, "as to read over my lines and hate them. I am one that 'gathers samphire, dreadful trade' — the Cliff of Poesy towers above me." He knew also the canker of pecuniary difficulty ("like a nettle leaf or two in your bed," his own expression is); and then, when he was but beginning his work, there fell on him the stroke of a mortal disease, recognized as such from almost the first moment. But in spite of all, and through it all, what a fire he kept burning! How gloriously happy he often was! He hungered and thirsted after beauty, and he had the blessedness that rewards such a craving. For blessedness (and that is the best of it) consists perfectly with a low estate and all manner of outward misfortune. It can do without gold, and even without health. As for resting in comforts and toys, easiness and fine clothes, a great aim, if it does nothing else for a man, will at least save him from that pitch of vulgarity. A great aim is of itself a great part of the true riches. As Keats said, having found it out early, "our prime objects are a refuge as well as a passion."

Such delight as the right men must always take in some of his letters! — especially, perhaps, some of the earlier ones, written in the period of his first fervors as a reader. He had never been a bookish boy (and no very serious harm done, it may be — for himself, at any rate, he was no believer in precocity), and now, when he fell all at once upon the great poets, it was as if he had been born again. What a relish he has! How he smacks his lips over a line of Shakespeare, — who "has left nothing to say about nothing or anything." Here was a poet who read the works of poets. Possibly if he had lived to be old, he might have changed his practice in this regard, finding his own works sufficient, as other elderly poets have before now been charged with doing. As it is, his raptures make one think again and again of Hazlitt's outburst, "The greatest pleasure in life is that of reading, while we are young;" which, if it does not hit the white, is at least well within the outer circle.[1]

His method was unblushingly epicurean. Like a bee in a field of flowers, he was always stopping to suck the sweet-

[1] At this very time, by-the-bye, Hazlitt was lecturing, and Keats, after hearing him, reports to his brother (February 14, 1818), "Hazlitt's last lecture was on Thomson, Cowper, and Crabbe. He praised Thomson and Cowper, but he gave Crabbe an unmerciful licking."

ness of a line. For that very purpose he was there. The happy boy! He had found out what books were made for. For a second time, nay, rather, for the first time, he had learned to read. A great discovery! — old as the hills and new as the morning. But new or old, a great discovery. For an intellectual youth there is none to match it, as there is no schoolmaster to teach it. And with what a gusto he describes the process! You would think he had found Aladdin's lamp. His fancy cannot see it from sides enough; as a child dances about a new toy, and can never be done with looking.

"I had an idea," he says, "that a man might pass a very pleasant life in this manner. Let him on a certain day read a certain page of full poesy or distilled prose, and let him wander with it, and muse upon it, and reflect from it, and bring home to it, and prophesy upon it, and dream upon it: until it becomes stale. But when will it do so? Never. When man has arrived at a certain ripeness in intellect, any one grand and spiritual passage serves him as a starting-post towards all 'the two-and-thirty palaces.' How happy is such a voyage of conception, what delicious diligent indolence! A doze upon a sofa does not hinder it, and a nap upon clover engenders ethereal finger-pointings; the prattle of a child gives it wings, and the converse of middle-age a strength to beat them; a strain of music conducts to 'an odd angle of the Isle,' and when the leaves whisper, it puts a girdle round the earth."

This he calls a "sparing touch of noble books." It is too much to be expected, of course, that readers in general, whose idea of intellectual delights is of a new novel every other day, should be contented with a method so parsimonious. If this is what you call epicureanism, they might say, pray count us among the Stoics. And for all that, as applied to Keats's own practice, "epicurean" was the right word.

What he would have been at forty or fifty, there is no telling. For the present he was not much concerned with whole poems as works of great constructive art. He was of an age to be (what Edward

FitzGerald is said to have always been) "more of a connoisseur than a critic, a taster of fragrant essences, an inhaler of subtle aromas." He loved beauty as at that stage he mostly found it (as the bee finds sweetness), in the individual flower, thinking far more of that than of the plant's symmetrical structure, or the composition of the landscape. In this particular he resembled Lamb, who, if he called himself "an author by fits," was no less truly a reader by fits. "I can vehemently applaud," he said with characteristic, half-true self-depreciation, "or perversely stickle, at *parts;* but I cannot grasp at a whole."

It was an admission of defect — he meant it so; but it is no slander to say that lovers of poetry are in general of substantially the same mind. Their taste is selective. They love short poems, or the beauties of long ones. Many of them have confessed as much, and many others could do no less were they called into the box. Lowell, whose standing as a critic nobody questions, though some may be bold enough, or "perverse" enough, now the man is dead, to rule him out of the class of poets, bids us remember how few long poems will bear consecutive reading. "For my part," he says, "I know of but one, — the 'Odyssey.'" And Samuel Johnson, who, great critic or not, had "a good deal of literature," told Boswell, "that from his earliest years he loved to read poetry, but hardly ever read any poem to an end."

The boy Keats, then, was not so utterly out of the way, at all events he was not without the support of good company, in taking for his own the motto of Ariel, —

"Where the bee sucks, there suck I."

And a good time he had of it; reading and idling, reading and writing, not too much in a hurry, no busier than a bee, following his bent, finding Shakespeare and the "Paradise Lost" every day greater wonders to him; looking upon fine phrases like a lover; more and more convinced that "fine writing, next to fine doing, is the top thing in the world."

"Next to fine doing," he said, — and meant it; for his life and his own doings chimed with the word. Nor does the word, even as a verbal confession of faith, stand alone. On the testimony of his friends, and on the testimony of his letters, Keats was no selfish weakling, no puny luxuriator in his own emotions, no mere hectic taster and maker of phrases. He worshiped beauty; he was born a poet, and rightly enough he followed his genius; but he was born also affectionate and generous; in his nature there was much of that glorious something which we call chivalry; and he knew as well as all the preachers could tell him that in any true assize high conduct must always bear away the palm. No more than the apostle of old had he any "poor vanity that works of genius were the first things. No! for that sort of probity and disinterestedness which such men as Bailey possess does hold and grasp the tiptop of any spiritual honors that can be paid to anything in this world." Truly said, of this world or any other; for many things may be great, but the greatest of all is charity.

It might almost have been expected that genius so sudden in its flowering, so amazingly exceptional, as Keats's, one of the wonders of human history, would be attended by some strain of disease, some taint, more or less pronounced, of mental or moral unsoundness. It is the more to be rejoiced in, therefore, that his nature, mental, moral, and physical (except for the tuberculosis which he doubtless contracted from his mother, over whom, in her last illness, he, a boy of fifteen, watched with all, a son's and daughter's faithfulness), was to all appearance eminently sane and normal. As a boy, undersized though he was, he would always be fighting (which is normal, surely), and as a man he showed habitually, with one distressing exception, a manly, self-respecting spirit.

The single exception has to do with his passion for Fanny Brawne, concerning which it may be enough to say that when a man is head over ears in love with a pretty girl, or a girl whom he thinks pretty, and is by her, or by some perversity of Fate, put off, he is *never* sane. The letters that Keats wrote to his inamorata may have been, as his friendly critic says, "the letters of a surgeon's apprentice."

For ourselves we will take the critic's word for it. We have never read them (in our opinion it was indecent or worse to print them), nor should we feel sure of our ability to tell in what respect the love letters of a young doctor might be expected to differ from those of a young schoolmaster or a young duke of the realm. To be crazy is to be crazy. Enough to say that they were not the letters of the poet Keats. Alas, alas! What a tragedy is human life! What a weak and silly thing is the human heart! A man sees a girl's face, and behold, he is no longer a reasonable being; his peace of mind is gone, his work hindered, his day shortened, his fame tarnished, his name a laughing-stock. It is that which hath been, and it is that which shall be. As was said of old, so one may feel like saying still, "A man hath no preëminence above a beast; for all is vanity."

And for all that, considering Keats's genius, its early development and its miraculous quality, and comparing him with men of his own kind, we must account him on the whole a man surprisingly well-balanced and sane. Call the roll of his famous poetic contemporaries, and few of them will be found saner. Good Archdeacon Bailey, who had abundant opportunity to know, said that common sense was "a conspicuous part of his character." Of how many of the others would it ever have occurred to any one to say the like?

He seems not to have been either crotchety or boastful, though he believed in aiming high, and made no scruple of professing, in so many words, that he "would rather fail than not be among the greatest." Born fighter that he was, born, too, of the *genus irritabile vatum* ("when I have any little vexation," he once wrote, with Lamb-like exaggeration, "it grows in five minutes into a theme for Sophocles"), he loved peace, and in the Biblical phrase pursued it, for which Mr. Arnold, it is pleasant to see, awards him full credit; but he was not to be trodden upon, he held the popular judgment of poetry in something like contempt (as all poets do, it is to be presumed), and he would not be crowded too hard even by the chiefest of his brethren. The most thoroughgoing Wordsworthian must read with amusement, if not with temptations to applause, the few clever sentences in which the youthful aspirant for poetic honors, in one of his letters, hits off some of that great man's foibles. He has no thought of denying Wordsworth's grandeur, he declares; but not for the sake of a few fine imaginative or domestic passages will he "be bullied into a certain philosophy engendered in the whims of an egoist." "Every man," he goes on, "has his speculations, but every man does not brood and peacock over them till he makes a false coinage and deceives himself. . . . We hate poetry that has a palpable design upon us, and, if we do not agree, seems to put its hand into its breeches pocket. Poetry should be great and unobtrusive, a thing which enters into one's soul, and does not startle it or amaze it with itself — but with its subject. How beautiful are the retired flowers! — how would they lose their beauty were they to throng into the highway, crying out, 'Admire me, I am a violet! Dote upon me, I am a primrose!'"

To another correspondent he expresses a fear that Wordsworth has gone away from town "rather huffed" about something or other, the nature of which does not precisely appear; but adds that he ought not to expect but that every man of worth should be "as proud as himself;" a remark concerning which we are bound to acknowledge, loyal Wordsworthians as within reason we esteem ourselves, that we rather like the sound of it.

An artist cannot well be without some of the defects — or what more steady-going, lower-flying people are wont to account the defects — that go naturally, if not of necessity, with the artistic temperament. For one thing, he must work more or less by fits and starts. Poems are not to be made — unless it be by a Southey — as a shoemaker makes shoes, so many strokes to the minute. It is a wonder how much Keats accomplished in his few years, and this even if we take no reckoning of his experiments and failures; but there were times, of course, when he could do nothing, and then, equally of course, he

A RELISH OF KEATS

could invent the prettiest kind of excuses for himself, excuses that were themselves hardly less than works of genius. At such a minute he would say, for instance, "Neither Poetry, nor Ambition, nor Love have any alertness of countenance as they pass by me; they seem rather like figures on a Greek vase." Or, if the beauty of the morning operated upon a sense of idleness, he would declare it "more noble to sit like Jove than to fly like Mercury." "Let us open our leaves like a flower," he would say, "and be passive and receptive; budding patiently under the eye of Apollo and taking hints from every noble insect that favors us with a visit. . . . I have not read any books — the Morning said I was right — I had no idea but of the Morning, and the Thrush said I was right — seeming to say, —

"'O fret not after knowledge — I have none,
And yet my song comes native with the warmth,
O fret not after knowledge — I have none,
And yet the Evening listens.'"

Not that he was ever foolish enough to despise knowledge, or trust overmuch to impulses "from a vernal wood," as if a poet could subsist on inspiration. A few weeks after the date of the letter just quoted, a letter which he himself qualified before he was done as "a mere sophistication," we find him renouncing a proposed pleasure trip. There is but one thing to prevent his going, he tells his correspondent. "I know nothing," he says, "I have read nothing, and I mean to follow Solomon's directions, 'Get learning, get understanding.' I find earlier days are gone by—I find that I can have no enjoyment in the world but continual drinking of knowledge. . . . There is but one way for me. The road lies through application, study, and thought. I will pursue it."

But as we counted it fortunate that he had already had the courage to forsake everything else for the pursuit of poetry, so we must be thankful that now, feeling his educational deficiencies, he did not do what nine professors out of ten, had he had the ill-fortune to consult them, would — very properly, no doubt — have advised him to do; that is to say, cease production for the time being and devote himself to study. That would have been a loss irreparable. His sun was so soon to go down! A mercy it was that he made hay while it shone.

For much of the hay that he made was as good as the sun ever shone on. That it was a short season's crop may pass unsaid. It is not within the possibilities of human nature, however miraculously endowed, to be mature at twenty-five. Enough, surely, if at that age a man has done a good bit of work of the rarest, divinest quality, work that, within its range and scope, the greatest and ripest genius could never dream of bettering. That is Keats's glory. So much as that one need not be either a poet or a critic to affirm; the critics and poets have agreed to affirm it for us. If Tennyson said, as reported, that "Keats, with his high spiritual vision, would have been, if he had lived, the greatest of us all; there is something magical and of the innermost soul of poetry in almost everything which he wrote;" and if Arnold put him, in two words, "with Shakespeare," why, then, for the present, at least, the case is judged, and we who are neither poets nor critics, but only tasters and relishers, can have no call to argue it.

So much being admitted, however, it is not to be assumed that here is an end of things. One may still like to talk a little. Hearing him praised, one may still say, —

> " ' 'T is so, 't is true,'
> And to the most of praise add something more."

Life would be a dull affair for the smaller men if comment and side remark were forever debarred as soon as the bigwigs had settled the main contention.

Leaving on one side, then, the odes and other pieces which by universal consent are perfect, or as nearly so as consists with human frailty,[1] let us content ourselves with intimating the profit which readers of a proper youthfulness and other needful, not over-critical, qualifications may

[1] We speak thus without forgetting that an American poet once wrote (what a reputable American periodical printed) a revised version of one of the odes, just to show how easily Keats could be improved upon. The good man might have been, though we believe he was not, brother to the one of whom we have all heard, who declared his opinion that there were n't ten men in Boston who could have written Shakespeare's plays.

derive from some of the other and longer poems, which by the same common consent, as well as by the acknowledgment of the man who wrote them, are in every sense imperfect.

Indeed, there are few things in Keats's letters more interesting in themselves, or more characteristic of their author, than his apologies for these same longer pieces, especially for "Endymion."

"Why endeavor after a long poem?" he has heard some one ask. And this is his answer: —

"Do not the lovers of poetry like to have a little region to wander in, where they may pick and choose, and in which the images are so numerous that many are forgotten and found new in a second reading; which may be food for a week's stroll in the summer? Do not they like this better than what they can read through before Mrs. Williams comes downstairs? a morning work at most."

Evidently his "lovers of poetry" are of the tribe of those whose practice we have heard him describing as "a sparing touch of noble books;" lovers rather than critics or students; browsers and ruminators; not determined upon devouring whole forests, or even entire trees, but content with getting here and there the goodness of a leaf or the sweetness of a blossom. He foresees that "Endymion" is doomed to be in one way a failure; he knows that his mind at present, in its nonage, is "like a pack of scattered cards." The words are his own. Yet he confides that there will be poetry in his long poem, and that the right spirits will find it. And so they do. He has touched their disposition to a nicety. They love to "wander in it." They may never have tried very hard to follow the story; they may not care to read any special student's supposed discoveries as to just how this part of the action is related to that or the other. But they like the poetry. They never read the poem, or read *in* it, without finding some. They do not wish it shorter, nor are they conscious of any very sharp regret that it is not better. Wisely or unwisely, they accept it as it is, and are thankful that the young man wrote it, and, having written it, took nobody's advice against printing

A RELISH OF KEATS

it. If they read *in* it, as we say, why, that is mostly what they do with the "Fairy Queen" and "Paradise Lost." It may be the fault of the poem, or it may be the fault of the reader; or it may be nobody's fault.

In the case of "Endymion," indeed, it requires no exceptional acumen to perceive that the work hangs feebly together, that its construction, its architectonic, if that be the word, is defective past all mending. "Utterly incoherent," is Mr. Arnold's dictum, and for ourselves we have no inclination to dispute him. Our fault or the poet's, we have always found it so. But like Mr. Arnold, we feel the breath of genius blowing through it, and therefore, as we say, we find in it not infrequently an hour of good reading.

Such reading, it has sometimes seemed to us (and the poet's apology, now we think of it, comes to much the same thing), is like walking in a forest, where we cannot see the wood for the trees. All about us they stand, dwindling away and away as we look, till, whichever way we turn, there is no looking farther.

Above our heads is a canopy of interlacing branches, —

> "overwove
> By many a summer's silent fingering," —

through which, densely as it is woven, steals here and there a sunbeam to play upon the carpet underneath. In such a place we know little and care less whither we may be going. Standing still is a good progress. Not a step but something offers itself, — a flower, a bed of moss, a trailing, berry-covered vine, a tuft of ferns. A brook talks to us, a bird sings to us, a vista invites us, a leafy spray, as we brush against it, whispers of beauty and the summer. These, and trifles like these, are what we could specify. All of them together do not make the forest, yet the least of them is not only part of the forest, but is what it is because of the forest. The soul of the forest speaks through it. How incomparably significant becomes of a sudden every common sound. If two branches but rub together, we must stop and listen. If a thrush whistles, we could stand forever to hear it. Not a sight or sound of them all would mean the same,

A RELISH OF KEATS

or anything like the same, if it were encountered in the open and by itself. It is the old lesson. The sparrow's note must come from the alder bough, the shell must be seen on the beach with the tide rippling over it.

And the magical verse, if it is to exercise its full charm, must be found, not in a book of extracts, nor as a fragment, but at home in its native surroundings. It must have been born in the poem, and we must discover it there! The poem which has made the verse must also have put us into the mood to receive it. How often have all readers found this true by its opposite. How often a line quoted is a line from which the glory seems to have departed, a line *dépaysé!* — as the tree, the bird, the leaf, if we see them in the open country and in the mood of the open country, can never be the same as if we saw them in the forest and in the mood which the forest induces.

We think, then, that the poet's plea is sound; that his long poem, whatever its shortcomings, is abundantly justified as a good place to wander about in; that there is poetry (one of the rare things of the world) in it which never would have been produced elsewhere, and which, now that it has been produced, can only be appreciated when read, as scientific men say, *in situ*. To transfer its beauties to a commonplace book would be like putting roses into a herbarium, or, more justly, perhaps, like setting a seashell on a parlor mantel.

In the long poem, too, as in the forest, though we were near forgetting to speak of it, there is always the chance of finding something unexpected; a line, an epithet, an image, that seems to have come into being since we were last here. Every perusal is thus a kind of voyage of discovery. It is as if the season had changed. New flowers have blossomed, new birds have come from the South, and the wood is a new place.

In all the work of genius, as we began by saying, there is no small part that seems to come from almost anywhere rather than from the mind and intention of the writer. And the more genius, we must believe, the more of this appearance of what is known (or unknown) as inspiration. Yet, in the case of Keats, a man of genius all compact, one has only to read his letters to see (and glad we must be to see it) that, for all his youthfulness and comparatively slight acquaintance with books, he was pretty well aware of himself, having withal a kind of philosophy of life and many shrewd ideas concerning the poetic art. His gift was no external, detachable thing, an influence of which he could give no account, and over which he had no control, like, shall we say, the inscrutable, uncanny, unrelated mathematical faculty of a Zerah Colburn, a thing by itself, significant of no general capacity on the part of its possessor. The man *himself* was a genius.

And being such, he was safest when he followed his own leadings. When he humbled himself to write what he hoped men would pay for, as, under pressure of his brother's and sister's need, he persuaded himself he might do ("the very corn which is now so beautiful, as if it had only took to ripening yesterday, is for the market; so, why should I be delicate?"), he was mostly wasting his time.

"I have great hope of success," he writes, "because I make use of my judgment more deliberately than I have yet done." It was a vain dependence. "Live and learn," says the proverb. And, prose men or poets, the brightest must mind the lesson. But Keats, alas! could not live. He was "born for death," and was already marked. His work, the best of it, was already finished. Racked and broken, devoured by the very madness of passion and wasting away with incurable disease, his tale henceforth is pure tragedy. If his passion was a weakness, — and no doubt it was, — to colder-blooded men a state of mind incredible, and to Pharisees and fools a thing to mock at, — so let us call it, and there be done. It was past cure, so much is certain. Here and there in his letters there are still gleams of brightness, sad touches of pleasantry. To his sister, about whose health he is continually in a fever, lest she should be going as his mother and his brother Tom have gone (and he himself far on the road), he is always a little improved, always making the most of the doctor's words of encouragement; but between times, to some other correspondent, he shows for a moment the plague that is consuming his life. It is heart-breaking to hear him. "If I had any chance of recovery, this passion would kill me." He cannot name the one of whom he is night and day thinking. "I am afraid to write to her — to receive a letter from her — to see her handwriting would break my heart." Even to see her name written would be more than he could bear. "Oh, Brown, I have coals of fire in my breast. It surprises me that the human heart is capable of containing and bearing so much misery."

And strange it is how cruel a price a man can be made to pay for what, at the worst, is only a piece of natural foolishness.

> "Well and wisely said the Greek,
> Be thou faithful, but not fond;
> To the altar's foot thy fellow seek,
> The Furies wait beyond."

Never man found this truer than Keats. There is but one letter more, — dated a month later, and addressed to the same friend. This time the dying man knows that he is taking leave, though he still quotes a doctor's soothing diagnosis. He is bringing his philosophy to bear, he says; if he recovers, he will do thus and so; but if not, all his faults will be forgiven. And then: "Write to George [his brother] as soon as you receive this, and tell him how I am, as far as you can guess; and also a note to my sister, who walks about my imagination like a ghost, she is so like Tom. I can scarcely bid you good-bye, even in a letter. I always made an awkward bow. God bless you!"

How wasteful is Nature! Once or twice in an age, one man out of millions, she brings forth a poet; and then, while his powers are still budding, she sends on them a sudden blight, and anon cuts him down. Wasteful, we say. But who can tell? Perhaps she also, like the rest of us, is doing what she can, and, like the rest of us, is disappointed when she fails.

ANATOLE FRANCE

ANATOLE FRANCE

M. Anatole France is a writer who is continually saying something. His thought is always breaking into bloom. He is not one of those who, on the ground of weightiness of matter, or other supposed excellence, have taken out a license to be dull. All his pages have light in them. His readers not only know in which direction they are going, — a great comfort, not always vouchsafed to such travelers, — but are made to enjoy the journey, having a thousand sights to look at by the way. It is an author's business, he considers, to make his truth beautiful; and nothing is beautiful but what is easy. An artist who knows his trade will "not so much exact attention as surprise it."

It sounds like a good creed; and the style of his writing answers to it. Its qualities are the classical French qualities, — neatness, precision, ease, moderation, lightness of touch, lucidity. In sum, it is such a style as comes of good breeding. He is clever without being smart, and pointed without emphasis. As for that dreadful something which goes by the name of rhetoric, you may search his twenty-odd volumes through without finding trace of it. His method is old-fashioned, his masters are the old masters. Brilliancy, surprise, felicities, originalities, — yes, indeed, he has all these and more, but he knows how to wear them They are all natural to him. "Elegant, facile, rapid," he says; "there you have the perfect politeness of a writer." Obscurity, difficulty, is to his way of thinking but a kind of bad manners.

He was born to enjoy beautiful things, one would say; elected before the cradle to a life of scholastic quietness and leisure: a dilettante and a saunterer, loving old streets, old shops, old books, the old literatures, fond of out-of-the-way and useless learning, the very type and pattern of an aimless reader and dreamer. And so, to take his word for it, he appears to have begun. Those were his best days. Then he was most himself. So, in certain moods, at least, it seems to him now. Of that time he is thinking when he says, "I lived happy years without writing. I led a contemplative and solitary life, the memory of which is still infinitely sweet to me. Then, as I studied nothing, I learned much. In fact, it is in strolling that one makes beautiful intellectual and moral discoveries."

The old book-stalls on the Paris quays, — one wonders how many scores of times he has an affectionate word to say for them in his various books. Even in one of the earlier essays of "La Vie Littéraire" he apologizes for what is already becoming a frequent reference. "Let me tell you," he breaks out, "that I can never pass over these quays without experiencing a trouble full of joy and sadness, because I was born here, because I spent my childhood here, and because the familiar faces that I saw here formerly are now forever vanished. I say this in spite of myself, from a habit of saying simply what I think, about that of which I think. One is never quite sincere without being a little wearisome. But I have a hope that, if I speak of myself, those who listen to me will think only of themselves; so that I shall please them while pleasing myself. I was brought up on this quay in the midst of books, by humble and simple people, of whose memory I am the only guardian. When I am gone they will be as if they had never been. My soul is all full of their relics."

He runs a risk of being wearisome, he says. But that is merely a grace-note of French politeness, to be taken as it is meant, and answered after its kind. Indeed, he knows better. It was he who said of Renan that his most charming book was his little volume of youthful reminiscence, because he had put most of himself into it. And of M. Anatole France it is equally true that although he has an abundance of ideas, and loves not only his own past but the past of the world, — especially of all mystics, heretics, skeptics, enthusiasts, and saints, — yet he never comes quite so close to his reader as when his talk grows most intimate. It is what we who read are always after, the man behind the pen. If he will really tell us about himself, about his inner, true self, which we blindly feel must be somehow very like another self, more interesting still, with which we seldom succeed in coming face to face, although, according to the accepted theory of things, it is, or ought to be, our nearest neighbor, — if he will really tell us something, little matter what, that is actually true about himself, we will sit up till morning to listen to him. It seems an easy way to be interesting, does it not? And so indeed it is, for the right man ; for the really fine things are always easy, — if one can do them at all.

There intrudes the doubt; for if success in personal reminiscence is easy, failure is ten times easier. Of course a man must have taste, an innate or well-bred sense of the fitness of things; and so a brook must have banks, to save it from degeneration and loss. But what if the stream itself be muddy, if it have no movement, no sparkle, no variety, if it do not by turns ripple over sunny shallows, loiter in comfortable eddies, and deepen and darken in dream-inviting pools? Or what if the banks be straight-cut and formal, till what should have been a brook is little better than a ditch? What if taste has become propriety, and propriety has hardened into primness, and the writing or the talk is without the breath of life? Yes, success is easy, and it is also impossible. As the art of man never made a mountain brook, so instruction never by itself made a writer. The rain must fall from heaven, and readability (and *hearability* likewise, since writing and talking are but two forms of the one thing) must come from the same source, or, as Emerson said, by nature.

If a man is to disclose himself, he must first have known something about himself, a pitch of intelligence by no means to be taken for granted; he must be one of the relatively few who are affectionately cognizant of their own feelings, who delight in their own view of things, who have felt, loved, suffered, and enjoyed, to whom life and the world have been inwardly real and interesting, for whom their own past especially is like a fair landscape, here in full sunshine, there flecked with shadows, but all a picture of loveliness and a thing to dream over.

In reminiscence, as in painting, the subject must be somewhat removed, loss of detail yielding a gain in beauty, since, in the one case, as in the other, what we seek is not an inventory, but a picture. This, or something like this, is what Renan had in mind when in beginning his "Souvenirs" he remarked that what a man says of himself is always poetry. For his own part, he declares, he has no thought of furnishing matter for *post-mortem* biographical sketches. He is going to tell the truth (mostly), but not the kind of truth of which biography is made. Biography and personal reminiscence are two things, and can never be written in the same tone. Many things, he tells us, have been put into his book on purpose to provoke a smile. If custom had permitted, he would more than once have written on the margin of the page: *cum grano salis*.

One thinks of Charles Lamb, though in general the two men had wonderfully little in common. How dearly he loved to talk of himself, hiding the while behind some modestly transparent veil of mystification! And how dearly we love to play the innocent game with him, seeing perfectly what is going on, but, as children do, making pretense of being deceived. Better than almost any one else he had the winsome gift of half-serious, tenderly humorous self-disclosure. As Renan said, it is all poetry, and always with something to smile at.

All this because of one of M. Anatole France's many stray bits of gossipy reminiscence concerning the old quays of Paris and his boyish adventures among them! Such trifles are characteristic; they connote other qualities, and of themselves show us one side of the man and the writer. He loves his own life, especially his real life, the happy years that lie behind him. The power to see them is to him a matter of wonderment, a kind of miracle, a true fairy's gift. If he could see the future with the same distinctness, the fact would be hardly more astonishing, and probably it would be much less beneficent. So he tells himself in one of those rare and precious moods when the soul seems preternaturally awake, and the commonest every-day objects wear a look of newness and mystery till we are taken with a kind of inward shivering as if we had been seeing ghosts.

For the more connected story of his youthful memories one must turn, of course, to the two volumes expressly devoted to them, "Le Livre de Mon Ami" and "Pierre Nozière." That he should have written *two* such books is significant of the hold that his childhood still has upon him. But the two are none too many. How delicious they are! — full of tenderness and humor, every sentence true to the pitch, and the writing perfect. And how many pictures they leave with us! The woman in white and her lover with the black whiskers. The ragged street urchin, Alphonse, whom the well-fed, well-dressed house boy envied and pitied by turns, till one day he (the good boy) pilfered a bunch of grapes from the sideboard, lowered them out of the window by a string, and called upon little Alphonse to take them; which the suspicious Alphonse proceeded to do with a sudden twitch at the cord (such rudeness!), after which, turning up his face to the window, he thrust out his tongue, put his thumb to his nose, and ran off with the dainty. "My little friends had not accustomed me to such fashions," the good boy confides to us. And then, to heighten his sense of disappointment (how commonly grown-up human benevolence is similarly disrewarded!), he bethought himself that he must tell his mother of his pious theft. She would chide him, he feared. And like a good mother she did, but with laughter in her eyes.

"'We ought to give away our own good things, not those of another,' she said; 'and we must know how to give.'

"'That is the secret of happiness,' added my father, 'and few know it.'

"He knew it, my father."

The books are full of such pictures, seen first by the child, and now seen again, losing nothing of their color, through the eyes of the man of forty; full, too, of a boy's dreams and ambitions. Now he will be a famous saint (like every boy, he is bound to be famous somehow), and instantly he sets about it with fastings, an improvised hair shirt, and even an attempt, ingloriously brought to nought by the strong arms of the housemaid, to play the rôle of Simeon Stylites in the kitchen. What with this muscular, unsympathetic maid, — who also tore his hair shirt from him, — and his father, equally unsympathetic, who pronounced him "stupid," the boy had a bad day of it, and by night-fall, as he says, "recognized that it is very difficult to be a saint while living with one's family. I understood why St. Anthony and St. Jerome went into the desert to dwell among lions and satyrs; and I resolved to retire the next day to a hermitage." And so he did, choosing a labyrinth in the neighboring Jardin des Plantes.

A few years later, wiser now and more worldly-minded, he is determined to set up catalogues like his old friend Father Le Beau; and soon (joy on the top of joy, and audacity almost past confession) he determines that he will some day print them, and *read the proofs!* Beyond that he can conceive of no higher felicity (though he has since learned, through the confidences of a blasé literary acquaintance, that "one wearies of everything in this world, even of correcting proofs!").

Needless to say, he did not become a cataloguer, more than he had become a saint; but good Father Le Beau, for all that, determined his boyish admirer's vocation, inspiring him with "a love for the things of the mind and with a weakness for writing;" inspiring him, also, with a passion for the past and with "ingenious curiosities," and, by the example of intellectual labor regularly performed without fatigue and without worry, filling him from childhood with a desire to work and instruct himself. "It is thanks to him," he concludes, "that I have become in my own way a great reader, a zealous annotator of ancient texts, and a scribbler of memoirs that will never see the light."

Good Father Le Beau! How plainly we can see him at his pleasant task, and the small boy beside him taking his lesson! And if any be ready to smile at the childish story, as if it were nothing *but* a childish story, — well, there is difference in readers. To some, let us hope, the simple adventures of a boy's mind, dreaming on things to come, will seem quite as entertaining, and even quite as instructive and morally profitable, as some more highly seasoned adventures of a man who covets his neighbor's wife, or a woman who covets her neighbor's husband.

Of books recounting the pleasures and miseries of illicit passion modern literature surely suffers no lack; and truth to tell, M. Anatole France himself (the more's the pity) has contributed to an already full stock two or three examples not easily to be outdone in piquancy of situation or freedom of speech. Concerning these no account is to be taken here. Enough to say that they are unspeakable, — in English, — though, not to do them injustice, it should be added that neither "Le Lys Rouge," nor even "Histoire Comique," for all its misleading, pleasant-sounding title, makes the path to the everlasting bonfire look in the remotest degree alluring. The old truth, old as man, that "to be carnally minded is death," is nowhere more convincingly set forth than in the modern French novel, whether it be Balzac's, Flaubert's, Maupassant's, Bourget's, or Anatole France's.

It is unfortunate, we must think, for our author's reputation and vogue outside of his own country, that not only the two of his books just now named, but at least three others, though in a less degree, are unfitted for full translation into English, or even to be left in their original tongue upon the open shelves of public libraries or on the family table. But what then? They were not written *virginibus puerisque*, their author would say, and even their freest parts treat of nothing worse than every newspaper is obliged somehow to chronicle, however it may veil its language, and nothing worse, perhaps, than is readily allowed in the English classics, especially in the books of the Bible and the writings of Shakespeare. Wonderful is the effect of time and distance! We gaze upon nude statues of the old Greeks and Romans without a shiver, but the representation of an American President bare only to the waist — as one may see, in all kinds of weather, poor unhappy-looking George Washington sitting in front of the national capitol — affects us with a painful sense of discomfort, not to say of positive indecency.

M. Anatole France, as has been said, seems by birth and early predilection to have been devoted to a career of studious leisure. He would always be contented, one would have thought, to be a looker-on at the game of life, sitting by the wayside, book in hand, and watching the world go past; taking it all as a show; never so much as considering the possibility of entering for any of the prizes that more ambitious men run for, nor concerned very much as to who should win or who lose ; hardly so much as an observer; a spectator rather, as he said himself; "in love," as he said again, "with the eternal illusion that wraps us round," but only as an illusion; cultivating his own garden, — like M. Bergeret, who delighted to cut the leaves of books, esteeming it wise to make for one's self pleasures appropriate to one's profession; at the most a collector of old books, and a teller of old tales; a lover of Virgil, a disciple of Epicurus, a friend of quietness, and a worshiper of the Graces.

Such we imagine M. Anatole France to have been when he wrote his earlier volumes, including the one which the majority of readers would probably name as the most beautiful of them all, "Le Crime de Sylvestre Bonnard." The dear old savant tells his own story, talking now to his cat, now to his friendly despot of a housekeeper, now to good Madame de Gabry, now, best of all, to himself. The whole story is, as it were, overheard by the reader, and surely there never was, nor ever will be, a prettier revelation of an old man's soul.

Like Renan, and like M. Anatole France, Sylvestre Bonnard, Member of the Institute, has a natural sense of humor, and if he does not put into his narrative things on purpose to make us smile, it is only because he is in no way thinking of us. He smiles often enough himself, his own oddities and blunders as an absent-minded scholar — since, like Cowper's Mr. Bull, he "has too much genius to have a good

ANATOLE FRANCE

memory" — providing him with abundant occasion; and we smile with him. We love him for his goodness, and we listen delighted to all his philosophy. If he is not a saint, he is something better, — or if not better, more interesting and lovable, — a man so humanly sweet, so simple-hearted, so pure-minded, so bright in his talk, so admirable in his kindness, so adorable a confesser of his own foibles, that there is no resisting him. Dear old celibate! — who had loved a pair of blue eyes in his youth, and had been true to their memory ever since! Verily, he had his reward. Never man awaited the sunset with a better grace.

The man who drew this character was surely at peace with the world and with himself. Life had so far been to him mostly a fair-weather stroll in a pleasant country. And the same may be said, with some grains of qualification, of the man who wrote the weekly articles that went to the making of the four volumes of "La Vie Littéraire." These are not things to last, it may be, like "Le Crime de Sylvestre Bonnard," which, if one may be so simple as to prophesy, can hardly fail to become a classic; but for the present they must afford to many readers, if not a keener, yet a more various, delight. They are books of extraordinary interest, in whatever light one may view them. As we turn them over, remarking here and there the pages that at different times have especially pleased us, we find ourselves saying again and again, Oh, that we had such books in English, and on English subjects! If there were in Great Britain or in the United States a writer who could, week by week, furnish one of our newspapers with pieces of literary criticism or bookish causerie of this enchanting quality; so light, so graceful, so original, so suggestive, so full of happy surprises, so bright with humor and philosophy, so perfect in form and temper, and so satisfying in substance! Yes, if there were! How quickly we would all subscribe for that newspaper! The articles might deal, as M. Anatole France's often do, with books that we have never read and have no thought of reading; it would not greatly matter. If the subject in hand were nothing but a text-book or an encyclopædia, a letter from an inquisitive correspondent, or a play of marionettes, the talk about it would be literature. And real literature, served to us fresh every Sunday morning! The very thought is an exhilaration. We are not to be understood as implying that excellent literary criticism is not more or less often written in English, and on both sides of the water. The question is not of moderately sound, reasonably instructive, workmanlike articles, proper enough to be read and forgotten, but of essays full of charm, full of genius, full of poetry, — essays in which, to adapt a saying of Thoreau, we do *not* miss the hue of the mind, essays that of themselves are in the truest sense little masterpieces of the literary art.

He had never thought of doing such things. His old publisher, Calmann Lévy, "rather friend than publisher," who had welcomed him in his obscurity, and smiled at his first humble successes, had for years been chiding his indolence and dunning him for another book. But he was in love with his idle ways and distrustful of his capacity. He was then living those "happy years without writing," of which we have seen him cherishing so fond a remembrance. But now came the manager of "Le Temps," a man accustomed to have his way, and behold, the dreamer's pen is again covering paper. "I believe you have a talisman," the new critic says to the editor, in dedicating to him the first of the four resulting volumes. "You do whatever you will. You have made of me a periodical and regular writer. You have triumphed over my indolence. You have utilized my reveries and coined my wits into gold. I hold you for an incomparable economist."

Such are the services of journalism to literature! A man never writes better, or more easily, than when regular work — not too pressing — keeps his hand in play. So Sir Walter Scott, hag-ridden by debt, if he finished a novel in the morning began another in the afternoon, because, as he explained, it was less difficult to keep the machine running than to start it again after a rest.

In this same dedicatory epistle to M.

Hébrard are to be found some of the brightest and most characteristic things that M. Anatole France has ever written about his own nature and habits, as well as about his ideas of critics and criticism. For talking about himself, as we have before said, and as the reader must have discovered even from our few quotations, he has the prettiest kind of talent. "You are very easy to live with," he tells M. Hébrard. "You never find fault with me. But I do not flatter myself. You saw at once that nothing great was to be expected, and that it was best not to torment me. For that reason you left me to say what I pleased. One day you remarked of me to a common friend, —

"'He is a mocking Benedictine.'

"We understand ourselves very imperfectly, but I think your definition is a good one. I seem to myself to be a philosophical monk. At heart I belong to an *abbaye de Thélème*, where the rule is comfortable and obedience easy, where one has no great degree of faith, perhaps, but is sure to be very pious."

There is nobody like a skeptic, he continues (he is echoing Montaigne), for always observing the moralities and being a good citizen. "A skeptic never rebels against existing laws, because he has no expectation that any power will be able to make good ones. He knows that much must be pardoned to the Republic;" that rulers at the best count for little; that, as Montaigne said, most things in this world do themselves, the Fates finding the way. Still he advises his manager never to confide his political columns to any Thelemite. The gentle spirit of melancholy that he would spread over everything would be a discouragement to honest readers. Ministers are not to be sustained by philosophy. "As for myself," he adds, "I maintain a suitable modesty and restrict myself to criticism."

And then, in two sentences, one of which has attained almost to the rank of a familiar quotation, he defines criticism and the critic.

"As I understand it, and as you allow me to practice it, criticism, like philosophy and history, is a sort of romance, and all romance, rightly taken, is an autobiography. The good critic is he who narrates the adventures of his own mind in its intercourse with masterpieces."

To be quite frank, he declares, the critic should begin his discourse by saying: "Gentlemen, I am going to speak about myself apropos of Shakespeare, apropos of Racine, or of Pascal, or of Goethe. It is a fine occasion."

And here, of course, the battle is joined between the two schools of critics: the subjective, or impressionistic, so called, on one side, and the objective, or scientific, so called, on the other.

Into this controversy (which, like many another, may yet turn out to be concerned with words rather than with things) we feel no call to enter. Like our author himself, we desire to maintain the modesty that is fitting to us. We content ourselves, therefore, with some random comments upon "La Vie Littéraire," which to our taste is one of the most delightfully readable books of recent times. Having read it and reread it, we are (somewhat ignorantly, to be sure, having nothing like an exhaustive acquaintance with universal current literature) very much of Mr. Edmund Gosse's opinion when he says of M. Anatole France that he is perhaps "the most interesting intelligence at this moment working in the field of letters." The word "perhaps," it will be noticed, is outside the double commas. A genuinely modest man likes to make a show of his modesty even in his use of quotations.

Whether criticism in general, as critics in general write it, ought to be of one school or another, subject to personal impression or subject to rule, one thing is beyond dispute: the singular charm, one feels almost like saying the incomparable charm, of "La Vie Littéraire" lies in its intimate, individual quality. It is not a set of formulas, nor even a thesaurus of literary opinions and estimates. It is the voice of a man, speaking as a man. As you listen, you see his mind at work; you know what he thinks about, and how he thinks about it; what he enjoys best and oftenest, what trains his reveries naturally fall into; how the world looks to him, past, present, and future. He does not set himself to reveal himself; when men do that, they mostly fail; his mind *plays* before you. Above all things, he is an ironist. There is nothing, least of all anything in himself or concerning himself, that he cannot smile at, though there may be tears in his eyes at the same moment. He admires, and can perfectly express his admiration; and when he despises, he is no more at a loss. The more he knows, the more he is ignorant, — and the more he wonders. He is full of modern knowledge, and he loves of all things a fairy tale. Shakespeare delights him, and he cannot say well enough nor times enough how greatly he enjoys the marionettes.

It can hardly have been an accident (and yet, for aught we know, it may have been, since accident often seems to be no more foolish than the rest of us) that his first "Times" essay was concerned with a representation of "Hamlet," and the second with the latest story of M. Jules Lemaître. Both the Danish prince and the martyr Sérénus were men oppressed and finally overcome by a sense of the mystery of things, having ideas, almost in excess, and being so skillful in debate that they could never come to a conclusion. Like horses and politicians, they needed blinders, and for lack of them could not keep a straight course.

Both make a lively appeal to our critic's sympathy. In his own way he is sufficiently like them. And so what ought, on one theory, to have been a dissertation upon Shakespeare's conception of Hamlet's character, runs of its own will into an address to the Dane himself. He is so real to the Frenchman that the two go home together, as it were, after the play, and the Frenchman, having sat silent so long, finds his heart full and his tongue suddenly unloosed.

First he must apologize to Hamlet for the audience, some part of which, as he may have noticed, seemed a trifle inattentive and light. Hamlet must not lay this to heart. "It was an audience of Frenchmen and Frenchwomen," he should remember. "You were not in evening dress, you had no amorous intrigue in the world of high finance, and you wore no flower in your buttonhole. For that reason the ladies coughed a little in their boxes while eating candied fruits. Your adventures could not interest them. They were not worldly adventures; they were only human adventures. Besides, you force people to think, and that is an offense which will never be pardoned to you here."

Still there were a few among the spectators who were profoundly moved, a few by whom the melancholy Dane is preferred before all other beings ever created by the breath of genius. The critic himself, by a happy chance, sat near one such, M. Auguste Dorchain. "He understands you, my prince, as he understands Racine, because he is himself a poet."

And then, after a little, he concludes by confiding to Hamlet what a mystery and contradiction the world continues to find him, though he is the universal man, the man of all times and all countries, though he is exactly like the rest of us, "a man living in the midst of universal evil." It is just because he is like the rest of us, indeed, that we find his character a thing so impossible to grasp. It is because we do not understand ourselves that we cannot understand him. His very inconsistencies and contradictions are the sign of his profound humanity. "You are prompt and slow, audacious and timid, benevolent and cruel; you believe and you doubt; you are wise, and above everything else you are insane. In a word, you live. Who of us does not resemble you in something? Who of us thinks without contradiction, and acts without inconsistency? Who of us is not insane? Who of us but says to you with a mixture of pity, of sympathy, of admiration, and of horror, 'Goodnight, sweet prince; and flights of angels sing thee to thy rest!'"

This may not be great Shakespearean criticism; certainly it bears no very striking resemblance to the ordinary German article that walks abroad under that name; but at least it is good reading, and so far as may be possible in a few sentences, it may be thought to go somewhat near to the heart of the matter.

As for the Sérénus of M. Jules Lemaître, he, too, is a thinker and dreamer set to live in difficult conditions. He, too, is caught in contradictory currents, and

finds it impossible to make the shore.
For him, as for Hamlet, death is the only
way out. His creator, of whom M. Anatole
France loves to talk, is himself a born
skeptic, always asking, under one ingenious form and another, the question of the
old Roman functionary, "What is truth?"
and never getting an answer. Like his
friend and critic, "he loves believers and
believes not." It may have been he of
whom it is remarked, somewhere, that
he has "a mind full of ironic curiosity."
We have been turning the volumes over
in search of the phrase. We did not find
it, but we found ourselves repeating the
word with which we began: "M. Anatole
France is a writer who is continually saying something." It seems to us truer than
ever; and it seems a considerable merit.

In the course of our search we fell
anew upon the essay dealing with that
amazing book, the "Journal" of the Goncourt brothers. It is no very enlivening
subject, one would say, but the essay is
of the brightest, sparkling from end to
end with those "good things" concerning
which the scientific critic may say what he

will, so long as the impressionistic critic will be kind enough to furnish them for our delectation. As plain untheoretical readers, we are thankful to be interested.

Of all books, as we know already, M. Anatole France believes in personal memoirs. In his opinion writers are seldom so likely to be well inspired as when they speak of themselves. La Fontaine's pigeon had good reason to say: —

> "Mon voyage dépeint
> Vous sera d'un plaisir extrême.
> Je dirai: 'J'étais là; telle chose m'avint:'
> Vous y croirez être vous-même."

Even a cold writer like Marmontel gets a hold upon us "as soon as he begins to tell about a little Limousin who read the Georgics in a garden where the bees were murmuring," — because he was the boy, and the bees were those whose honey he ate, the same which he saw his aunt warming in the hollow of her hand, and refreshing with a drop of wine, when the cold had benumbed them. As for St. Augustine's "Confessions," so called, our essayist has no very exalted opinion of them. The great doctor, he thinks, hardly confesses enough. Worse yet, he hates his sins; and, in the way of literature, "nothing spoils a confession like repentance."

But Rousseau, " poor great Jean-Jacques," "whose soul held so many miseries and grandeurs," — he surely made no half-hearted confession. "He acknowledged his own faults and those of other people with marvelous facility. It cost him nothing to tell the truth. However vile and ignoble it might be, he knew that he could render it touching and beautiful. He had secrets for that, the secrets of genius, which, like fire, purifies everything."

But we must be done with quotation, though the matter that offers itself is fairly without end. Especially one would be glad to cite some of the essayist's reminiscences of the men he has known: some of them famous, like Flaubert, "a pessimist full of enthusiasm," who "had the good part of the things of this world, in that he could admire;" Jules Sandeau, whom the critic, when a child, used to meet on the quays of Paris, which are "the adopted country of all men of thought and taste;" and dear old Barbey d'Aurévilly, so queerly dressed, so profane a believer, "so frightfully Satanic and so adorably childish;" and others, — and these among the best, — two or three priests, in particular, — never heard of except in our author's pages.

One would like, also, to speak of his favorite heterodox theory touching the fallible nature of posterity as a judge of works of art; of the fun that he pokes so effectively at the new school of symbolists and decadents (small wonder they do not love him); of his ideas upon language, upon history, upon the grossness of Zola, — with which he as an artist has no patience, — upon the exalted rank of the critical essay, upon the educational value of the humanities. These and many other things have their place in the four volumes, and every one is touched with grace and something of originality. Everywhere the personal note makes itself heard. It is a voice, not the scratching of a pen, that we listen to, the voice of a man who never forgets that he was once a child. He has lived in Eden. We all begin, he tells himself, where Adam began. "In those blessed hours," he says, "I have seen thistles springing up amid heaps of stones in little sunny streets where birds were singing; and I tell you the truth, it was Paradise."

The two or three years during which he was contributing weekly articles to "Le Temps" were not quite of this heavenly quality, we may safely presume; in the inevitable course of things the gates of Eden must for some time have been already closed against him; but if one is to judge by his books of the period, meaning to include among them "La Rôtisserie de la Reine Pédauque," "Les Opinions de M. Jérôme Coignard," and "Le Jardin d'Épicure," — three of the best and most characteristic, though the two first named are not for readers afflicted with what a French critic calls *pudeur livresque*, — they were still years of quietness and a reasonably full content. He was writing and studying more than formerly, to be sure, and of course, by his own showing, was learning so much the less; but, taking everything into account, he and the world, for all its badness, were pulling pretty well together.

Since then, somehow, we cannot profess to know exactly how or why, a change appears to have come over him; a change not altogether for the worse, nor altogether for the better. Life, in his eyes, is no longer so bright as it was. He is more serious, more satirical, less disposed to mind his rhyme and let the river run under the bridge; a little out of conceit with his old rôle of saunterer and looker-on. He seems to have heard a drum-beat, and if there is to be a fight, he will, after a rather independent fashion of his own, bear a hand in it. Perhaps this is the manlier part. At all events, there is no quarreling with it, and the evil days on which Anatole France has fallen ("*le perfide Anatole France*," as we are told that his political enemies — a strange word for use in connection with the author of "Sylvestre Bonnard" and "Le Jardin d'Épicure" — are accustomed to call him) have borne their full share of fruit.

His second manner, to call it so, is like

his first in this regard, that its most successful creation is an old scholar. M. Bergeret is Sylvestre Bonnard with a difference, as the present Anatole France is the old Anatole France with a difference. It strikes us as almost a pleasantry of Fate that these two leading characters should stand thus as representatives of their creator's two selves, or, if one prefers to express it so, of their creator's one self in his two periods of calm and storm.

Sylvestre Bonnard's life ran an even course. Its incidents were no more than the windings and falls of a quiet brook, — just enough to keep it wholesomely alive and give it a desirable diversity and picturesqueness. The world was good to him; and he thanked it. If he did not marry the girl with the pair of blue eyes, — the eyes *de pervenche*, — he was happier in his bachelorhood than the majority of men are in their married condition, and doubly happy toward the last, when time and chance (with more or less of human assistance) brought him his heart's desire in the opportunity to care for his lost Clementine's grandchild. His professional successes were according to his taste: he was a member of the Institute, an authority upon ancient texts, and in his old age the happy author of a book upon a new hobby.

Such was the life of a savant as M. Anatole France conceived it before the world was too much with him, before "Nationalists" and "Royalists" had begun to look askance upon him, and call him traitor.

M. Bergeret, like M. Bonnard, is a man of kindly nature, a scholar, and a lover of peace, but life to him, as to Shelley, has been "dealt in another measure;" a disloyal wife, uncongenial daughters, squalor in his house, disappointment in his calling, lack of favor with his colleagues and superiors, and, to fill his cup, the Dreyfus controversy, which makes him a target for stoning.

And in the midst of it all, notwithstanding it all, what a dear old soul, and what an interesting talker! — so amiably philosophical, so keen in his thrusts, so sly in his humor, so fond of good company, his own and his dog's included, and, in spite of his weaknesses, so equal to the occasion! If he is irreligious, according to his neighbors' standards, it is at least "with decency and good taste."

The four volumes in which he figures ("Histoire Contemporaine," they are jointly called), like all the works of their author, are crammed with clever sayings. There is no great story, of course, though some of the incidents are many shades too lively to be set in modest English type; but the characterization and the dialogue are of the best, — in the good Yankee sense of the word, "complete."

For its full appreciation the book — it is really one, in spite of its four titles — demands a more familiar acquaintance with the ins and outs of current French politics than the average American reader is likely to bring to it. There are so many wheels within wheels, and the intrigues are made, of set purpose on the author's part, to turn upon desires and considerations so almost incredibly sordid and petty! It is a comedy; we are bound to laugh; but it is also a horror, and is meant to be. Satire was never more biting. The game of provincial politics, bishop-making and all, is played with merciless particularity before the reader's eyes; and if he fails to follow some of the moves with perfect intelligence, he sees only too well the smallness and baseness and cruelty of the whole; a game in which a matron's honor is no more than a pawn upon the chessboard, to be given and taken without so much as an extra pulse-beat, even an extra pulse-beat of her own. If it be true, or within a thousand miles of true, — well, to repeat the saying of one of old, a critic accounted wise in his day, "man hath no preëminence above a beast!"

Poor M. Bergeret! He ought to have been so happy! Like his human creator, he was born for life in a cloister, some Abbaye de Thélème, where he should have had nothing to do but to read his books, say his prayers, mind a few cabbages, perhaps, and be quiet; and instead of that, here he is passing his days in such a turmoil that he experiences a kind of joy on finding himself in the street, the one place where he gets a taste of "that sweetest of good things, philosophical liberty." And with all the rest of his tribulations there falls upon him that dreadful nightmare of the Dreyfus case. Neither he nor his neighbors can let it alone. It is like the bitterness of aloes in all their conversation.

One resource he still has; one neighbor, better still, one housemate, with whom he can discuss anything, even the "Affaire," with no risk of being stoned or misunderstood. His dog Riquet, though he "does not understand irony" (a congenital deficiency, it must have been, with such opportunities), is to our *Maître de Conférences à la Faculté des Lettres* a true friend in need. For that matter, indeed, M. Bergeret is probably not the only man who has found it one of the best points in a dog's favor that you can say to him anything you please. If your human neighbor stands in perishing need of wholesome truth, or if you stand in sore need of expressing it to him, and if there happens to be some not unnatural unwillingness on his part, or some momentary lack of courage on yours, why, you have only to deliver your message to him vicariously, as it were, to the sensible relief of your own mind, if not to the edification of his.

"Riquet," said M. Bergeret, after a vain endeavor to make one of his brother provincials submit himself to reason, "Riquet, your velvety ears hear not him who speaks best, but him who speaks loudest." And Riquet, well used to his master's conversational eccentricities, took the compliment in good part; in much better part, at all events, than any human interlocutor would have been likely to take it. For really, unless one actually lost one's temper, one could not say just that to a neighbor and equal, especially if it happened to be true.

For a heretic living among the orthodox there is nothing like keeping a dog. So we were ready to say and leave it; but we bethink ourselves in season that there is a more excellent way. Keep a dog, if you will, but keep also the pen of a novelist. Then all your beliefs and half beliefs and unbeliefs, all your benevolently contemptuous opinions of men and of men's institutions, all your treasures of irony and satire, dear as these ever are to the man who possesses them, instead of being wasted upon a pair of velvety ears, may be trumpeted to the world at large through the lips of a third party, a "character," so called, some M. Bergeret, if you can invent him, or an Abbé Coignard.

It is one of the best reasons for reading fiction, by the way, provided it is written by a man of insight and force, that he is so much more likely to tell us what he thinks when he is not compelled to speak in his own person.

A happy lot is the novelist's. Such a more than angelic liberty as he enjoys, so comfortably irresponsible and blameless as he is, whatever happens! One thinks again of Jérome Coignard, concerning whom too little is finding its way into this paper. That grand old Christian and reprobate, as we know, could live pretty much as he listed, and hold pretty much such "opinions" as pleased him, at ease all the while in the assurance that somewhere in a deep inner closet, fast under lock and key, he preserved a faith in the Christian mysteries so perfect and unsoiled — never having been subjected to any earthly contact — that the good St. Peter, when the inevitable time should come, would be sure to pass its possessor into the good place without a question.

Yet it will never do for us to intimate that M. Anatole France has sought to save either comfort or reputation by talking through a mask. His theological, political, and socialistic heresies, if you call them such, this being matter of opinion, have been too openly expounded, and have brought him, as has already been told, too many enemies and reproaches. The most that we started to say under this head was that the storms into which the currents of the world have drifted him are reflected in his "Histoire Contemporaine," especially in the difference between his M. Bergeret and his M. Bonnard.

Of the two, M. Bergeret has the greater philosophic interest for us, as well as the greater number of rememberable things to say to us. If the reader wishes to see him in two highly contrasted situations, let him turn to the wonderful chapter describing his sensations and behavior immediately after detecting his wife's infidelity, and the beautiful one in which he and his more practical sister visit together the old Paris mansion in which they had passed some portion of their childhood. They were house-hunting at the time, and the Master, falling into one of his far-away, philosophical moods, remarked, apropos of something or nothing: "Time is a pure idea, and space is no more real than time." "That may be so," answered his matter-of-fact, executive-minded sister, "but it costs more in Paris."

Doctor Johnson called himself "an old struggler," and the words come unbidden into our minds as we review M. Bergeret's story. To us, we must confess, the old Latin professor seems almost as real a personage as the Great Cham of literature himself. We hope he is happy in his new post of honor at the Sorbonne. It was time, surely, that some of the quails and the manna should be found in his basket.

And now it is pleasant to add, by way of ending, that the latest book of M. Anatole France seems to indicate that he also, as well as the man of his creation, has come out into a larger place. His mood is quieter and less satirical, though he is still many degrees more serious than in the old days of "Thaïs" and "Sylvestre Bonnard." "Sur la Pierre Blanche" is a work of the rarest distinction; not a book for the casual reader to hurry over in pursuit of a story (in a loose way of speaking it may be characterized as a volume of imaginary conversations), but one to be cherished and dwelt upon by such as love the perfection of art and are not averse to knowing what kind of thoughts visit a free-thinking, humanity-loving man, of a philosophical, half-conservative, half-radical turn of mind, in these days of social and political unrest, as he looks back upon the origins of Christianity and forward into those new and presumably brighter eras which we who live now may dream of, but never see.

The motto of the book explains the significance of its title: "You seem to have slept upon the white stone amongst the people of dreams." Toleration, the spread of peace, imperialism, the socialistic evolution (following hard upon the capitalistic evolution, now at its height, or passing), the yellow peril, so called, the white peril, the future of Africa, — these are some of the larger and timelier questions considered. In general, the thoughts of the book are those of a scholar whose face is turned toward practical issues. The author is not concerned with any Utopia, — absolute justice, by his theory, being not a thing to be so much as hoped for, — but with some quite possible amelioration of the existing order, and some gradual, natural, irresistible approaches (irresistible because they are the work of Nature herself) toward a state of society less unequal, not to say less unendurable, than the present.

Let those scoff who will; for ourselves we rejoice to see the man, like the boy, "dreaming on things to come."

At the same time, we should not be sorry to believe that, in the heat of writing, and out of the love, natural to all of us, of making facts conform to theory, we may have laid a thought too much of emphasis upon the alterations through which his mind has passed. His days, we suspect, have, after all, been pretty closely bound each to each by natural piety. We recall his fine saying about Renan, brought up in the Roman Church and dying an unbeliever, that he changed little. "He was like his native land, where clouds float across the sky, but the soil is of granite, and oaks are deeply rooted."

Changed or unchanged, in his first manner or his second, Republican or Nationalist, socialist, anti-imperialist, "intellectual," or what not, who will refuse to read a writer who can express himself after such a fashion?

VERBAL MAGIC

VERBAL MAGIC

A MUSIC-LOVER and devoted concert-goer of my acquaintance — "uninstructed, but sensitive," to characterize him in his own words — is accustomed to say that he distinguishes several kinds of enjoyable music. One kind is interesting: here he puts the work of composers so unlike as Berlioz and Brahms. Another kind is exciting; under which head he ranks the greater part of Wagner and the Bach fugues! And still another kind is charming. Whenever he uses this last epithet, he adds an explanation, the word being now so worn by indiscriminate handling as hardly to pass by itself at its full face value. He means that the music thus described — heavenly music, he sometimes calls it (of which his typical example seems to be Schubert's unfinished symphony) — has upon him an indescribable ravishing effect, as if it really and literally charmed him. Exactly why this should be, he does not profess to decide. All such compositions are highly melodious and in some good degree simple; but then there is plenty of other excellent music to which the same terms seem to be equally applicable, which nevertheless lays him under no such spell. "I don't undertake to explain it," he says; "so far as I am concerned, it is all a matter of feeling."

Analogous to this is my own experience — and, I suppose, that of readers in general — with certain fragments of poetry, which have for me an ineffable and apparently inexhaustible charm. Other poetry is beautiful, enjoyable, stimulating, everything that poetry ought to be, except that it lacks this final something which, not to leave it absolutely without a name, we may call magic. Whatever it be called, it pertains not to any poet's work as a whole, nor in strictness, I think, to any poem as a whole, but to single verses or couplets. And to draw the line still closer, verse of this magical quality — though here, to be sure, I may be disclosing nothing but my own intellectual limitations — is discoverable only in the work of a certain few poets.

The secret of the charm is past finding out: so I like to believe, at all events. Magic is magic; if it could be explained, it would be something else; to use the word is to confess the thing beyond us. Such verses were never written to order or by force of will, since genius and our old friend — or enemy — "an infinite capacity for taking pains," so far from being one, are not even distantly related. The poet himself could never tell how such perfection was wrought or whence it came; nor is its natural history to be made out by any critic. The best we can do with it is to enjoy it, thankful to have our souls refreshed and our taste purified by its "heavenly alchemy;" as the best that our musical friend can do with the unfinished symphony is to surrender himself to its fascination, and be carried by it, as I have heard him more than once express himself, up to "heaven's gate."

And yet it is not in human nature to forego the asking of questions. The mind will have its inquisitive moods, and sometimes it loves to play, in a kind of make-believe, with mysteries which it has no thought of solving, — a harmless and perhaps not unprofitable exercise, if entered upon modestly and pursued without illusions. We may wonder over things that interest us, and even go so far as to talk about them, though we have no expectation of saying anything either new or final.

Take, then, the famous lines from Wordsworth's "Solitary Reaper:" —

> "Will no one tell me what she sings? —
> Perhaps the plaintive numbers flow
> For old, unhappy, far-off things,
> And battles long ago."

The final couplet of this stanza is a typical example of what is here meant by verbal magic. I am heartily of Mr. Swinburne's mind when he says of it, "In the whole expanse of poetry there can hardly be two verses of more perfect and profound and exalted beauty;" although my own slender acquaintance with literature as a whole would not have justified me in so sweeping a mode of speech. The utmost that I could have ventured to say would have been that I knew of no lines more supremely,

VERBAL MAGIC

indescribably, perennially beautiful. Nor can I sympathize with Mr. Courthope in his contention that the lines are nothing in themselves, but depend for their "high quality" upon their association with the image of the solitary reaper. On such a point the human consciousness may possibly not be infallible; but at all events, it is the best ground we have to go on, and unless I am strangely deluded, my own delight is in the verses themselves, and not merely nor mainly in their setting. Yet of what cheap and common materials they are composed, and how artlessly they are put together! Nine every-day words, such as any farmer might use, not a fine word among them, following each other in the most unstudied manner — and the result perfection!

By the side of this example let us put another, equally familiar, from Shakespeare: —

> "We are such stuff
> As dreams are made on, and our little life
> Is rounded with a sleep."

Here, too, all the elements are of the plainest and commonest; and yet these few short, homely words, every one in its natural prose order, and not over-musical, — "such stuff" and "little life" being almost cacophonous, — have a magical force, if I may presume for once to speak in Mr. Swinburne's tone, unsurpassable in the whole range of literature. We hear them, if we *do* hear them, and all things earthly seem to melt and vanish.

Not unlike them in their sudden effectiveness is a casual expression of Burke's. For in prose also, and even in a political pamphlet, if the pamphleteer have a genius for words, an inspired and unexpected phrase (and inspired phrases are always unexpected, that being one mark of their divinity) may take the spirit captive. Thus, while Burke is talking about the troubles of the time, being now in the opposition, and blaming the government as in duty bound, suddenly he lets fall the words, "Rank, and office, and title, and all the solemn plausibilities of the world;" and for me, I know not whether others may be similarly affected, politics and government are gone, an "insubstantial pageant faded." "All the solemn plausibilities of the world," I say to myself, and for the present, though I am hardly beyond the first page of the pamphlet, I care not to read further; like Emerson at the play, who had ears for nothing more after Hamlet's question to the ghost: —

> "What may this mean,
> That thou, dead corse, again in complete steel
> Revisit'st thus the glimpses of the moon?"

I am writing simply as a lover of poetry, "uninstructed, but sensitive," not as a critic, having no semblance of claim to that exalted title,—among the very highest, to my thinking, as the men who wear it worthily are among the rarest; great critics, to this date, having been fewer even than great poets; but I believe, or think I believe, in the saying of one of the brightest of modern Frenchmen: "Le bon critique est celui qui raconte les aventures de son âme au milieu des chefs-d'œuvre." So I delight in this adventure of Emerson's mind in the midst of "Hamlet," as I do also in a similar one of Wordsworth's, who was wont to say, as reported by Hazlitt, that he could read Milton's description of Satan —

> "Nor appeared
> Less than Archangel ruined, and the excess
> Of glory obscured" —

till he felt "a certain faintness come over his mind from a sense of beauty and grandeur."

One thing, surely, we may say about verse of this miraculous quality: it does not appeal first or principally to the ear; it is almost never rich in melodic beauty, as such beauty is commonly estimated. It is musical, no doubt, but after a secret manner of its own. Alliteration, assonance, a pleasing alternation and interchange of vowel sounds, all such crafty niceties are hidden, if not absent altogether, — so completely hidden that the reader never thinks of them as either present or absent.[1] The appeal is to the imagination, not to the ear, and more is suggested than said. Such lines, along with their simplicity of language, may well have something of mysteriousness. Yet they must not puzzle the mind. The mystery must not be of the

[1] Is there a possible connection between this fact and the further one that really magical lines are seldom or never to be found in the work of the more distinctively musical poets, — say in Coleridge, Shelley, Tennyson, and Swinburne?

VERBAL MAGIC

smaller sort, that provokes questions. If the curiosity is teased in the slightest to discover what the words mean, the spell is broken. There is no enchantment in a riddle.

Neither is there charm in an epigram, be it never so happy, nor in any conceit or play upon words.

> "I could not love thee, Dear! so much,
> Loved I not Honor more," —

nothing of this kind, perfect as it is, will answer the test. Mere cleverness might compass a thing like that. Indeed, the very cleverness of it, its courtly gracefulness, its *manner* (one seems to see the bodily inflection and the wave of the hand that go with the phrase), the spice of smartness in it, are enough to remove it instantly out of the magic circle. Magical verse is neither pretty nor clever. It speaks not of itself. If you think of *it*, the charm has failed.

In my own case, in lines that are magical to me, the suggestion or picture is generally of something remote from the present, a calling up of deeds long done and men long vanished, or else a foreboding of that future day when *all* things will be past; a suggestion or picture that brings an instant soberness, — reverie, melancholy, what you will, — that is the most delicious fruit of recollection. It suits with this idea that the verse has mostly a slow, meditative movement, produced, if the reader chooses to pick it to pieces, by long vowels and natural pauses, or by final and initial consonants standing opposite each other, and, between them, holding the words apart; such a movement as that of the Wordsworth couplet first quoted, —

> "For old, unhappy, far-off things,
> And battles long ago," —

or as that of the still more familiar slow-running line from the sonnets of Shakespeare, —

"Bare ruin'd choirs, where late the sweet birds sang," —

a movement that not merely harmonizes with the complexion of the thought, but heightens it to an extraordinary degree. Not that the poet wrote with that end consciously in view, or altered a syllable to secure it. Wordsworth's lines, it is

VERBAL MAGIC

safe guessing, were for this time given to him, and dropped upon the paper as they are, faultless beyond even his too meddlesome desire to alter and amend. Indeed, in this as in all the best verse, it is not the metrical structure that produces the imaginative result, but exactly the opposite.

And here, as I think, we may gather a hint as to the impassable gulf that separates inspired poetry from the very highest verse of the next lower order. Take such a dainty bit of musical craftiness as this, the first that offers itself for the purpose: —

> "The splendor falls on castle walls
> And snowy summits old in story:
> The long light shakes across the lakes,
> And the wild cataract leaps in glory.
> Blow, bugle, blow, set the wild echoes flying,
> Blow, bugle; answer, echoes, dying, dying, dying."

Admirable after its kind, a kind of which it might seem unfair to say that less is meant than meets the ear; but set it beside the Wordsworth couplet, so easy, so simple, —

> "Without all ornament, itself and true," —

so inevitable and yet so impossible. One is cheap in its materials, but divine in its birth and in its effect; the other is made of rare and costly stuffs, but when all is done it *is* made. Though it sound old-fashioned to say so, there is no art like inspiration.

The supreme achievement of poetic genius is not the writing of beautiful passages, but the conception and evolution of great poems, — the whole, even in a work of the imagination, being greater than any of its parts; but poetic inspiration reaches its highest jet, if we may so speak, its ultimate bloom, in occasional lines of transcendent and, as human judgment goes, perfect loveliness. I should like to see a rigorously sifted collection of such fragments, an anthology of magical verse, nothing less than magic being admitted. It would be a small volume, —

"Infinite riches in a little room;"

but it would need an inspired reader to make it.

QUOTABILITY

QUOTABILITY

THERE is a kind of writing by which the reader is led along, perhaps hurried along, if it be a narrative, without pause from beginning to end. Everything follows directly from what has gone before; the mind is held upon the same level of interest; and the impression produced is, as it were, a single impression. There is another kind of writing, which brings the reader now and then to a halt. He looks up from the page, perhaps, fixing his eyes upon vacancy, and turning the thought, or the expression of it, over in his mind; or he betakes himself to a book of extracts and conveys a sentence or two into its keeping; or, possibly, if he is one of the rare ones who buy books and read with pencil in hand, he may indite a note on the margin of the leaf, or at least set a mark there, — as one blazes a tree at the foot of which treasure is buried. The author has said something, — something in particular, fresh, surprising, original; something that seems to have come from his own mind; a thing to be pondered over and returned upon. For the moment there is no going further; the reader has turned thinker, or is lost in a dream. It is as if a man had been walking down a pleasant road bordered with hedges and fields, one much like another, and now of a sudden has rounded a corner, and sees before him a lake or a waterfall, something new, different, unexpected, at the sight of which he stops as by instinct. Or you may say, it is as if a man had been traveling steadily forward, thinking only of his journey's end, and all at once catches the shine of a gold piece in the path, or sees by the wayside a flower so novel and beautiful that it must be stepped aside for and looked at.

We have had in America three writers, living in the same country village at the same time, who exemplified in a really striking manner these two styles of writing: Hawthorne on the one hand, and Emerson and Thoreau on the other.

Hawthorne's work you may read from end to end without the temptation to transfer so much as a line to the commonplace book. The road has taken you through many interesting scenes, and past many a beautiful landscape; you may have felt much and learned much; you might be glad to turn back straightway and travel the course over again; but you will have picked up no coin or jewel to put away in a cabinet. This characteristic of Hawthorne is the more noteworthy because of the moral quality of his work. A mere story-teller may naturally keep his narrative on the go, as we say, — that is one of the chief secrets of his art; but Hawthorne was not a mere story-teller. He was a moralist, — Emerson himself hardly more so; yet he has never a moral sentence. The fact is, he did not make sentences; he made books. The story, not the sentence, nor even the paragraph or the chapter, was the unit. The general truth — the moral — informed the work. Not only was it not affixed as a label; it was not given anywhere a direct and separable verbal expression. If the story does not convey it to you, you will never get it. Hawthorne, in short, was what, for lack of a better word, we may call a literary artist.

Emerson and Thoreau, on the other hand, were journalizers. Their life was not to create, but to think, to see, to read, and to set down the results of it all, day by day. When Emerson would make a piece of literature, — a lecture, or an essay, or even a book, — he sought out related paragraphs from his diary, dovetailed them together, disguising the joints more or less successfully, as might happen, — it was no great matter, — added collateral ideas as they occurred to him, and the job was done. It was done the more easily because the journal was not a receptacle for impressions hastily noted. Sentence and paragraph had been assiduously finished to a word, turned this way and that and settled finally into shape, before they went into it; for a journal, with him, was not a collection of rough jewels, but a drawer full of pearls and precious stones, each carefully cut and polished, ready for the setting or the string.

And what was true of Emerson was true in good degree of Thoreau, who followed the same general method, but with a less pronounced and continuous effect of discontinuity: partly, it would appear, because of a difference in the turn of his mind (more given to reason, and less to intuition), and partly because of the narrative form into which his natural historical bent almost of necessity carried him, — a form by which pages and whole chapters of his work are held pretty closely together.

If with Hawthorne we put Irving, — who was like him so far as the point now under consideration is concerned, fluidity of style and an absence of "passages," — we have four of our American classics in well-contrasted pairs. One pair, we may say, did work that was like tapestry, woven throughout; the other's product was rather like patchwork, — composed of rare and valuable stuff, but still patchwork.

This comparison, be it understood, is not to be taken as an attempt to settle a question of comparative rank. A contrast is not of itself an appraisal, nor a figure of speech an end of the argument.

And after all, if figures of speech are to be regarded, a floor of tiles may be as beautiful, and even as "artistic," as the finest of woven carpets. Let comparisons go. We may study differences without exalting one or depreciating another. Of the four writers now named, we are not to say that any one was greater than all the rest. Each had his superiorities and his inferiorities, the second necessary concomitants of the first; for every virtue casts its shadow.

Emerson, for his part, seems to have been keenly aware of the disconnectedness of his work, — his "formidable tendency to the lapidary style," he terms it, — and even to have accepted it as a defect. "I dot evermore in my endless journal, a line on every knowable in nature," he writes to Carlyle; "but the arrangement loiters long, and I get a brick-kiln instead of a house." That was one face of the medal; but his "bricks" are now of more value than many another man's streetful of buildings.

Thoreau, though he too had his humble moods, was in general more self-reliant

— or at least more self-assertive — than his older friend and master. He *believed* in the "lapidary style," or in some wholesome approach to it; and what he believed in he would stand up for. "We hear it complained of some works of genius," he says, "that they have fine thoughts, but are irregular and have no flow. But even the mountain peaks on the horizon are, to the eye of science, parts of one range." He is defending Emerson, — though he does not name him, — and, indirectly, himself; and with the same end in view he goes on to praise Sir Walter Raleigh, whose style, he says, has a natural emphasis, like a man's tread, "and a breathing space between the sentences." And he declares, correctly enough, that what the ignorant applaud as a "flow" of style is much of it nothing but a "rapid trot."

One thing is certain: a man must work according to his own method. For him that is the best method, and indeed the only one. Carlyle entreated Emerson to "become concrete, and write in prose the straightest way." "I wish you would take an American Hero, one whom you really love; and give us a History of him,—make an artistic bronze statue (in good *words*) of his Life and him. I do indeed." Thoreau's appeal to Emerson is for exactly the opposite: less art, if need be, and less concreteness, but more "far-off heats," more "star-dust and undissolvable nebulæ." To that end he turns Emerson's own verse against him. "From *his*

> 'lips of cunning fell
> The thrilling Delphic oracle.'

And yet sometimes,—

> We should not mind if on our ear there fell
> Some less of cunning, more of oracle."

Clever critics, both of them, the Scotchman and the Yankee; but meanwhile, between the two fires, Emerson kept on polishing pearls and cutting cameos, with hardly so much as an attempt at an "artistic bronze statue." The author of the essay on "Self-Reliance" knew that a man must work with his own mind, as he must wear his own face; that no method is so good or so bad but that it may be damaged by an attempt to make it as good as another's.

QUOTABILITY

And admirable as artistic perfection and absolute unity are, there remains a place, and a high place, for works of another order. All the world, even the stickler for classical perfection, loves a good sentence. Blessed is the writer who now and then makes one. We forgive him for carelessness of construction, and, almost, for every other literary fault, if once in a while — not *too* infrequently — he packs wit or wisdom into a score or so of memorable words.

In speaking of a quotable style, we are not thinking of works like the Wisdom of Solomon, the Meditations of Marcus Aurelius, and the Thoughts of Pascal and Joubert, books that are nothing but collections of maxims and aphorisms; nor even of books like Bacon's Essays or Amiel's Journal, that come near to falling under the same head. To find a happy and pregnant sentence in such a place is like taking an apple out of a dish and eating it at the table; to run upon one in the reading of a *book* is like plucking an apple from a wayside tree in the midst of a half-day ramble, and munching it on the road.

The fruit may be as fair and well-flavored in the first case as in the second, but what a difference in the relish of it! It is one thing to receive a coin over the banker's counter, and another to pick a nugget out of the gravel. In reading, as well as anywhere else, a man enjoys the thrill of discovery.

Here, in great part, lies the enduring charm of an author like Montaigne, who wrote without plan, rambling at his own sweet will, never sticking to his text, and never so much as dreaming of unity or anything else that could be called "artistic," yet making a book to live forever. As Sainte-Beuve says, you may open it at what page you will, and be in what mood you may, and you are sure to find a wise thought expressed in lively and durable phrase, a beautiful meaning set in a single strong line. And the best of it all is that these fine sentences, so detachable and memorable, are written like all the rest of the essay, and are part and parcel of it. No attention is called to them; they call no attention to themselves. They drop on the page, and the pen runs on.

QUOTABILITY

Seemingly, it was as easy for the writer to set down a "durable" phrase — done once for all and past all bettering — as to mention the kind of fish he preferred or any other trivial every-day matter. His good things are never tainted with smartness, the besetting vice of sentence-makers in general, nor have they at all the appearance of things designed to nudge the reader, to keep him awake, as if the writer had said to himself, "Go to, let us brighten up the discussion a bit."

A gift of this sort comes mostly by nature, but no one ever wrote much and well without arriving at some pretty definite notions as to the art of writing; and so it was with Montaigne. If his style was discursive, formless, highly sententious, and yet to an extraordinary degree familiar, he was not only aware of the fact, but gloried in it. He loved a natural and plain way of speaking, he tells us; the same on paper as in the mouth; juicy and sinewy (*succulent et nerveux*), irregular, incontinuous and bold, every piece a body by itself, — "a soldier-like style." Fine words he had no place for. "May I never use any other language than what is used in the markets of Paris!" he exclaims. As for mere rhetoric, he held it cheap, as every good writer does. Word painting, no matter how well done, is "easily obscured by the lustre of a simple truth." But a good sentence, a thing worth saying and well said, he believed to be always in order. "If it is not good for what went before nor for what comes after, it is good in itself." He praises Tacitus for being "full of sentences." And therein, perhaps, as in Thoreau's eulogy of Sir Walter Raleigh, we may see the author defending his own practice. There is no neater way of speaking well of ourselves than by complimenting our own special virtues in the person of another. In truth, however, Montaigne had no need to apologize even with indirectness. His "good sentences" are not only good in themselves, but good for what precedes and follows. They are never stuck on nor thrust in. On the contrary, as has been already observed, they are sure to be part of the very substance of the essay itself. You will never find Montaigne writing or retaining a paragraph for the sake of its snapper, like those authors of whom he said that they would "go a mile out of their way to run after a fine word."

There is a natural relation, it would seem, between a quotable style and a fondness for quoting. If a man's own thought falls easily into well-minted, separable phrases, he will almost of course be appreciative of similar aphoristic turns of speech in the works of others. So we find Montaigne's pages bespattered from top to bottom with extracts from the philosophers and poets of an older time. As years passed, and successive editions of the book were published, the quotations grew more and more numerous, till some of the essays seemed in danger of losing their identity and becoming hardly more than leaves out of a commonplace book.

And as it was with the Frenchman, so was it with our two Concord philosophers, Emerson and Thoreau. They were almost as fond of others' bright things as of their own. And the same may be said of their contemporary and critic, Lowell, who, like them, was also a master of the phrase, a putter forth of "stamped sentences," like gold and silver coins, as one of his admirers has called them. He, too, is always offering us a nugget out of another man's pack. All three of these men, be it added, borrowed not only with freedom, but with great advantage to their own work. They had a right to borrow, being in good measure original in their very quotations, because, as has been remarked of Montaigne, "they employed them only when they found in them an idea of their own, or had been struck by them in a new and singular manner."

But what a change when we turn to Hawthorne! His work is all of a piece, woven in his own loom. As nobody quotes him, so he quotes nobody. Inverted commas are as scarce on his pages as November violets are in the Concord meadows. You will find them, but you will have to search for them. On Thoreau's page they are thick as violets in May.

We were not undertaking to determine rank or to appraise values, we said, but so much as this we will venture upon suggesting: that a piece of pure art —

"The Scarlet Letter," if you will — is not on that ground alone to be considered as worthier in itself, or better assured of lasting honor, than some work less perfectly constructed, but, it may be, more nobly inspired. In the final result of things, literary merit and literary fame are not portioned out by any critical yardstick. Lowell complained of Thoreau that "he had no artistic power such as controls a great work to the serene balance of completeness." True enough. It is the same criticism which Carlyle, and Arnold after him, brought against Emerson; in whose case, also, we need not dispute the point. But Lowell said further of Thoreau, "His work gives me the feeling of a sky full of stars;" and again: "As we read him, it seems as if all-out-of-doors had kept a diary and become its own Montaigne. . . . Compared with his, all other books of similar aim, even White's 'Selborne,' seem dry as a country clergyman's meteorological journal in an old almanac." In other words, Thoreau was not an artist, but he did something new, and something grandly worth doing. Emerson, likewise, was not an artist; but the critic who tells us so tells us in the same breath that Emerson's essays are the most important work done in English prose during their century.

Whether Emerson will outlive Hawthorne, or Hawthorne outlive Emerson, who can say? It would be rash guessing to attempt a prophecy. As for Thoreau, there are some, perhaps, who would bid higher for his chance of immortality than for that of either of his two famous townsmen.

Let such things turn out as they may, Emerson and Thoreau have each given to American literature, and better still to American life, something that can never be lost, even though their works and their names together should be forgotten; and they have done this partly by reason of their very limitations, their making of sentences and paragraphs — portable wisdom — instead of "artistic bronze statues." "Wisdom is the principal thing," said an ancient writer; and an English critic and statesman of our own day has uttered the same truth in more modern fashion. "Aphorism or maxim," says Mr. John Morley, "let us remember that this wisdom of life is the true salt of literature; that those books, at least in prose, are most nourishing which are most richly stored with it; and that it is one of the main objects, apart from the mere acquisition of knowledge, which men ought to seek in the reading of books."

Yes, and it is one of the objects that men do seek; for the history of literature proves abundantly that the world keeps a relish for that which feeds the soul as well as for that which ministers to the passion for beauty; if it crowns the literary artist, it has a wreath also for his humbler brother — if he *is* humbler — the originator and disseminator of thought. For it is to be considered that a man with a genius for writing is not therefore a man of original ideas, or indeed, so far as the necessity of the case goes, of any ideas at all. His gift may be — nay, perhaps is likely to be — purely artistic and literary, a faculty for seeing and describing. Thus we read of Sterne that he was a great author, "not because of great thoughts, for there is scarcely a sentence in his writings which can be called a thought, . . . but because of his wonderful sympathy with and wonderful power of representing simple human nature." Obviously, it is not to such as he that we are to go in search of wisdom. The man who furnishes us with that commodity, the quotable man, be his rank higher or lower, is one who thinks, or, lacking that, has an instinct for the discovery and expression of thought, — a man under the friction of whose pen ideas crystallize into handy and final shape, and so become current coin.

THE GRACE OF OBSCURITY

THE GRACE OF OBSCURITY

CLEARNESS, directness, ease, precision, — these are literary virtues of a homely and primary sort. Reserve, urbanity, depth, force, suggestiveness, — these, too, are virtues, and happy the writer who has them. He is master of his art.

No good workman likes to be praised overmuch for the elementary qualities. Let some things be taken for granted, or touched upon lightly. Tell a schoolboy that he writes grammatically, — if you can, — but not the editor of a newspaper. Almost as well confide to your banker that you hold him for something better than a thief. "Simplicity be cursed!" a sensitive writer used to exclaim, as book after book elicited the same good-natured verdict. "They mean that I am simple, easily seen through. Henceforth I will be muddy, seeing it is beyond me to be deep." But nature is inexorable, and with the next book it was the same story. Probably there is not a line of his work over which any two readers ever disputed as to its meaning. In vain shall such a man dream of immortality. Great books, books to which readers return, books that win vogue and maintain it, books for the study of which societies are organized and about which libraries accumulate, must be of a less flimsy texture, — in his own testy phrase, less "easily seen through."

Consider the great classics of all races, the Bibles of the world. Not one but abounds in dark sayings. What another book the Hebrew Scriptures would be if the same text could never be interpreted in more than one way, if some texts could ever be interpreted at all! How much less matter for preaching! How much less motive for exegetical research! And withal, how much less appeal to the deepest of human instincts, the passion for the vague, the far away, and the mysterious!

All religious teachers, in so far as they are competent and sincere, address themselves to this instinct. The worthier they are of their calling, the better do they appreciate the value of paradox and parable.

THE GRACE OF OBSCURITY

The greatest of them made open profession of his purpose to speak over the heads of his hearers; and his followers are still true to his example in that particular, however they may have improved upon it in other respects. They no longer encourage evil by turning the other cheek to the smiter; not many of them foster indolence by selling all that they have and giving to the poor; but without exception they speak things hard to be understood. Therein, in part at least, lies their power; for mankind craves a religion, a revelation of the unseen and the unprovable, and is not to be put off with simple morality, with such commonplace and worldly things as honesty, industry, purity, and brotherly love. No church ever waxed great by the inculcation of these humble, earthly, every-day virtues.

In literature, the value of half-lights is recognized, consciously or not, by all who dabble in foreign tongues. Indeed, so far, at least, as amateurs are concerned, it is one of the chief encouragements to linguistic studies, the heightened pleasure of reading in a language but half understood.

The imagination is put freshly in play, and time-worn thoughts and too familiar sentiments are again almost as good as new. Doudan, writing to a friend in trouble, drops suddenly into English, with a sentence or two about the universality of misfortune. "Commonplaces regain their truth in a strange language," he explains; "if we complain of ordinary evils, we ought to do it in Latin." The hint is worth taking. So long as we have something novel and important to communicate, we may choose the simplest words. "Clearness is the ornament of profound thoughts," says Vauvenargues; but we need not go quite so far as the same philosopher when he bids us reject all thoughts that are "too feeble to bear a simple expression." That would be to reduce the literary product unduly. Joubert is a more comforting adviser. "Banish from words all uncertainty of meaning," he says, "and you have made an end of poetry and eloquence." "It is a great art," he adds, "the art of being agreeably ambiguous."

Such tributes to the vague are the more significant as coming from Frenchmen, who, of all people, may be said to worship

THE GRACE OF OBSCURITY 315

lucidity. Let us add, then, the testimony of one of the younger French writers, a man of our own day. "Humanity hardly attaches itself with passion to any works of poetry and art," says M. Anatole France, "unless some parts of them are obscure and susceptible of diverse interpretations." And in another place in the same volume ("Le Jardin d'Épicure") we come upon this fine saying: "What life has of the best is the idea it gives us of an unknown something which is not in it." How true that is of literature, also! The best thing we derive from a book is something that the author never quite succeeded in putting into it. What good reader (and without good reading there is no good writing) has not found a glimpse, a momentary brightness as of something infinitely far off, more exciting and memorable than whole pages of crystalline description?

Vagueness like this is one of the noblest gifts of a writer. Artifice cannot compass it. If a man would have it, let him pray for a soul, and refresh himself continually with dreams and high imaginings. Then if, in addition, he have genius, knowledge, and literary tact, there may be hope for him. But even then the page must find the reader.

Of vagueness of a lower order there is always plenty; some of it a matter of individual temperament, some of it a matter of art, and some a matter of a want of art. It is not to be despised, perhaps, since it has utility and a marketable value. It results in the formation of clubs, and so is promotive of social intercourse. It makes it worth men's while to read the same book twice, or even thrice, and so is of use in relieving the tedium of the world. It renders unspeakable service to worthy people who would fain have a fine taste in literature, but for whom, as yet, it is more absorbing to guess riddles than to read poems; and it is almost as good as a corruption of the text to the favored few who have an eye for invisible meanings, — men like the famous French philosopher who discovered extraordinary beauty in certain profundities of Pascal, which turned out to be errors of a copyist.

This inferior kind of obscurity, like most things of a secondary rank, is open to cultivation, although the greater number of

THE GRACE OF OBSCURITY

those who profit by such husbandry are slow to acknowledge the obligation. A bright exception is found in Thoreau. He was one who believed in telling the truth. "I do not suppose that I have attained to obscurity," he writes. But he was too modest by half. He did attain to it, and in both kinds : sometimes in willful paradox and exaggeration, a sort of "Come, now, good reader, no falling asleep!" and sometimes, but less often, — for such visitations are rare with the best of men, — in some quick, unstudied phrase that opens, as it were, an unsuspected door within us, and makes us forget for the time being both the author and his book.

Perhaps it would be true to say that when men are most inspired, their speech becomes most like Nature's own, — inarticulate, and so capable of expressing things inexpressible. What book, what line of verse, ever evoked those unutterable feelings — feelings beyond even the *thought* of utterance — that are wakened in us now and then, in divinely favorable moments, by the plash of waters or the sighing of winds ? When an author does aught of this kind for us, we must love and praise him, let his shortcomings be what they will. If a man is great enough in himself, or serviceable enough to us, we need not insist upon all the minor perfections.

For the rest, these things remain true: language is the work of the people, and belongs to the people, however lexicographers and grammarians may codify, and possibly, in rare instances, improve it. Commonplaces are the staple of literature. The great books appeal to men as men, not as scholars. A fog is not a cloud, though a man with his feet in the mud may hug himself and say, "Look, how I soar!" Preciosity is good for those that like it; they have their reward; but to set up a conventicle, with passwords and a private creed, is not to found a religion. In the long run, nothing is supremely beautiful but genuine simplicity, which may be a perfection of nature or the perfection of art; and the only obscurity that suits with it and sets it off is occasional, unexpected, momentary, — a sudden excess of light that flashes and is gone, surprising the writer first, and afterward the reader.

IN DEFENSE OF THE TRAVELER'S NOTE-BOOK

IN DEFENSE OF THE TRAVELER'S NOTE-BOOK

It is a more or less common habit of Americans to cry out against the conceit of foreigners, Englishmen especially, who, after a run through "the States," publish their impressions of the country. These outcries — though that may seem too strong a word — are supposed to be quite independent of the character of the comments in question, whether favorable or unfavorable. In the tourist's eyes, Americans may be an uninteresting, boastful, worldly-minded people. The magnitude of our lakes may not blind him to the imperfections of our newspapers, and in spite of Niagara and the prairies, he may esteem our politicians, for the most part, a vulgar and time-serving set. Whatever criticisms of this sort he in his unwisdom may feel called upon to express are likely to have their modicum of truth; at least they would have, if any one but a foreigner were to utter them. Americans are not slow to say similar things of each other, and especially of their public men. Except on the Fourth of July, we are far from constituting anything fairly to be called a mutual admiration society. The complaint, then, is not that the tourist offers criticism of such and such a tenor, but that he takes it upon himself to offer any criticism at all. What business has he with "impressions of America" after a visit of a month or two? And even if he has impressions, why should he be so presumptuous as to print them? A great people cannot be understood after this haphazard, percursory fashion. True; but the objection is futile, if for no other reason, because it goes wide of the mark. The question is not of understanding a people, but of having something to say about them.

Since the world began, men have traveled, and, having traveled, have recounted their adventures. The two things go together, and are alike inevitable. And the thing that hath been, it is that which shall be. Some authors travel in other men's books; some travel in the outward and literal sense of the word; and both tell as good a story as they can of the wonders they have seen. It is only here and there a philosopher who can sit at home and spin his web out of his own insides. Thoreau delighted to talk as if Concord were the centre and sum of the world. Everything grew there, everything happened there. Why should a Concord man ever stir beyond the town limits? Sure enough! And yet what are Thoreau's books but records of his journeys: "A Week on the Concord and Merrimack Rivers;" "The Maine Woods;" "Cape Cod;" "A Yankee in Canada;" "Excursions." With him, as with the rest of us, it was the volume he had just read that he liked to talk about; it was the country he had just seen that his pen naturally busied itself with describing. Even his one Concord book is really a book of travels. To write it he went into camp, that he might study the world on its off side, as it were, and feel his life new.

In other words, for here we come to the pith of the matter, it is the fresh impression that is vivid, and therefore will have itself expressed. We may almost say that it is the only thing that can be expressed. This is what Bagehot had in mind. "Those who know a place or a person best," he said, "are not those most likely to describe it best; their knowledge is so familiar that they cannot bring it out in words." And this truth, partial though it be, and, like all truth, liable to misunderstanding and abuse, is the scribbling tourist's encouragement, and, if he be supposed to need it, his perennial justification.

More than one scholar has failed to produce the great work that was expected of him, — that he of all men seemed elected to produce, — simply because he put off the doing of it till his knowledge should be something like complete. So monumental a structure could not be too carefully prepared for, he thought: a conscientiousness most scholarly and honorable, but deadly in its result; for by the time he had laid in his stores, he had lost the freshness of his enthusiasm; a palsy had stricken his pen; and by and by the night came, and his knowledge perished with him.

Writers of travels, whatever their shortcomings, fall into no error of this kind.

They strike while the iron is hot; and whether their subject be Africa or America, that is the true method. The value of such literature depends on the observer's alertness, fairness, good sense, and general competency, rather than upon the length and leisureliness of his journey. Time of itself never did much for a blind man's vision; and to come back to our Englishman, he may run through America in a month, or spend a year in his note-taking, and in either event he will discover only what he came prepared to discover. If the photographic plate is sensitive enough, it may need but the briefest exposure. And anyhow, let the picture turn out never so badly, no irreparable harm is done. The object itself is not altered because its portrait is drawn awry. What we have to dread is not the foreigner's unfair opinion of us, but our unfair opinion of the foreigner. It is our own thoughts that do us injury, not other men's thoughts about us. And if this be too rare an atmosphere for comfortable every-day breathing, we may come at a similar result on lower ground. Who are we, that we should be treated better than the rest of the world? Must our feelings never be hurt, because we are Americans? Have we never learned that it is a man's part to be thankful for intelligent and friendly criticism, and to bear all other in silence?

Let visitors to "the States," then, be "impressed;" and let them print their impressions, the more the better. Some of them will be shallow, some of them unkindly and prejudiced, some, perhaps, ignorantly and foolishly eulogistic. We shall be blamed for faults that are beyond our mending, and praised for virtues that were never ours, — if such virtues there be. At best, the criticism and the comment will fall a little short of inerrancy; for perfection is one of the lost arts, even in England; but in the sum many true things will be said, and in the end the cause of truth will be forwarded; and possibly, if a thousand English pens are thus employed, one of them may happen to make an immortal picture of the Great Republic as it now is, and as it will not be, for better or worse, a hundred years hence. Thus it is, at any rate, by one lucky experimenter out of many, that immortal work is done.

Some critics, it is true, would have literature, even current literature, to consist solely of such happy strokes. Let no man write anything till he can write a masterpiece, they say. Yes, and let no boy go near the water till he has learned to swim; and since crows have waxed destructive, let cornfields be planted hereafter with no outside rows; and lest malarial fevers should make an end of the human race, let all plains and valleys be filled up, and nothing remain but mountains. In short, seeing that failure has been the rule hitherto, let us abolish rules, and get on with exceptions alone; a condition of things curiously prefigured in certain Grammars of the Latin Language, of a kind still sorrowfully remembered by elderly people. A fine economy, surely, and well worth thinking about. But for the time being, till dreams become substantial, this present evil world, as we reverently call it, remembering its Creator, must be suffered to jog along in its ancient, expensive, wasteful-seeming, happy-go-lucky, highly-exception-able manner: a million seeds, and one tree; a million books, and one *chef-d'œuvre*. Classics are not yet produced of set purpose, nor do they make their advent in royal isolation, starred and wearing the laurel. They come, as was said just now, with the crowd, the "spawn of the press," if they come at all, and are only sifted out by the slow hand of time. And meanwhile their humbler fellows, missing of immortality, may nevertheless have their day and serve their turn. Readers, fortunately or unfortunately, are of many grades, and even the wisest of them — in some unwiser but not infrequent mood — desire not a classic, but something a shade less excellent. "There is no book that is acceptable, unless at certain seasons." So said Milton; and the saying is true, even of "Paradise Lost." In the great sea of literature there is room both for the big fish and for "the other fry." Let us be thankful; and if we are scribblers, by nature or by conceit, let us scribble on.

CONCERNING THE LACK OF AN
AMERICAN LITERATURE

CONCERNING THE LACK OF AN AMERICAN LITERATURE

"Writers who have no past are pretty sure of having no future." — LOWELL.

IT is an old story that the people of the United States have been slow in achieving their intellectual independence. The British yoke has remained upon our minds, though we have cast it off our necks. Our literary men, especially, have deferred to English models and English ideas. So we have been told till the tale has become monotonous.

What everybody says must be true — perhaps; but even so, there may be something to offer on the other side, or by way of extenuation, although the man who should venture to offer it — such is the peculiarity of the case and the perversity of human nature — might find himself accounted unpatriotic for coming to the defense of his own countrymen.

In times past, assuredly, whatever may

be true now, the condition of things so much complained of was little reprehensible. Good or bad, it was nothing more than was to have been expected as circumstances then were. We had been English to begin with, and, for better or worse, the English nature is not of a sort to be put off with a turn of the hand, at the signing of a political document. It is self-evident, also, that in the world of ideas every people, whether it will or no, must live largely upon its ancestry. The utmost that any generation can hope to do is to contribute its mite to the intellectual tradition. The better part of its reading must be out of books that its predecessors have sifted from the mass and handed down. If it adds a few of its own — two or three, by good luck — to the permanent literature of the race, it does all that can reasonably be demanded of it. And even so much as this was hardly to be looked for from the American people during its colonial period and for some decades afterwards, with a wilderness to be subdued, savage neighbors to be held in check, and all the machinery of civiliza-

LACK OF AMERICAN LITERATURE 333

tion to be newly set up. Books are a record and criticism of life, and those to whom life itself is an absorbing occupation are not likely, unless they are almost insanely intellectual, to spend any very considerable share of their days in work of a secondary and postponable character. Life is more than criticism, and the best and greatest people are those whose deeds give other people something to write about. It is not to be wondered at, therefore, if American books of a kind to be called literature were slow in coming; and we may confess without shame that up to the year 1820 or thereabouts—say till the advent of Irving and Cooper—the people of this country, if they read anything better than sermons and almanacs, were obliged to depend chiefly upon foreign authors. To which confession it may be added, equally without shame, that even the works of Cooper and Irving were scarcely sufficient of themselves to satisfy for many years together the cravings of eager and serious minds. At all times and in all countries, such minds, with the best will in the world to be loyal to their own day, have been obliged to look mainly to old books.

About the past, then, we need not spend time in mourning. If we play our part as well as the fathers played theirs, we shall have no great cause to blush. Since their day, what with Irving and Cooper and their contemporaries and successors, there has been no dearth of books written on this side of the water; but the complaint is still rife that we have little or nothing in the way of a national literature: by which it is meant, apparently, that our writers are not yet Americans, or do not succeed in expressing the national spirit. Only the other day, a critic, discoursing on "the conservatism and timidity of our literature," charged it against Lowell that "in his habits of writing he continued English tradition," whatever that may mean. "Our best scholar" allowed his real self to speak but twice, we are given to understand; then he spoke in dialect. His "Commemoration Ode" was a splendid failure, because it was "imitative and secondary." Whether it, too, should have been written in dialect, we are not informed; but it appears to be taken for granted that its failure, if it was a failure, came, not from lack of genius or inspiration, but from deference to foreign models. One cannot help wondering what Lowell himself would have said to such a criticism: that he wrote in English and like an Englishman because he dared not write in his own tongue and in his own way. When a Scotchman complimented him upon his English, — "so like a native's," — and asked him bluntly where he got it, he answered with equal bluntness, in the words of the old song, —

"'I got it in my mither's wame.'"

Yet Lowell, who spoke but twice in his own character, seems to have done better than most of his fellows; for he and Curtis are the only men of letters to find a place in a recent "Calendar of Great Americans." All their contemporaries and predecessors were either not great, or else were something other than American, — cosmopolitan, provincial, or English. Irving, Cooper, Poe, Bryant, Hawthorne, Longfellow, Emerson, Whittier, Holmes, Prescott, Motley, Bancroft, Parkman, —

not one of these will bear the test. As for Emerson, he is ruled out by name, because he was the "author of such thought as might have been native to any clime." He is of the world, and therefore not American. It seems a hard judgment that the man who wrote "The Fortune of the Republic," "The Young American," and the "Concord Hymn," — the man of whom it was recently said, so finely and so truly, that "he sent ten thousand sons to the war," — should find himself at this late hour a man without a country. On such terms it is doubtful praise to be called a cosmopolitan; and in view of such a ruling it becomes evident that the exact nature of Americanism as a literary quality is yet to be defined. Lowell's attempt in that direction, by-the-bye, is probably among the best. An American, according to Lowell's idea of him, — so Mr. James says, — was a man at once fresh and ripe.

When it comes to practice, however, there is one American poet whose literary patriotism was never called in question. The reference is of course to Whitman. Listen to him, as he appeals to whoever "would assume a place to teach or be a poet here in the States:"—

> "Who are you indeed who would talk or sing to America?
> Have you studied out the land, its idioms and men?
> Have you learned the physiology, phrenology, politics, geography, pride, freedom, friendship of the land? its substratums and objects?
> Have you considered the organic compact of the first day of the first year of Independence, signed by the Commissioners, ratified by the States, and read by Washington at the head of the army?
> Have you possessed yourself of the Federal Constitution?
> Do you see who have left all feudal processes and poems behind them, and assumed the poems and processes of Democracy?"

"Conservatism and timidity"! Here is one man, at all events, who is not to be accused of "continuing English tradition." He, if nobody else, breathes a "haughty defiance of the Year One." He may or may not be "ripe;" he certainly is "fresh." If there be some who fail to enjoy his verse, there can be none who do not admire his courage.

But surely it was not to be insisted upon, nor even expected, that all American authors should break away thus suddenly and completely from the past. Perhaps it was not even to be desired: partly because variety is better than the best of sameness, and partly because so abrupt a change might in the long run have hindered our emancipation. Some readers would have been puzzled, others would have been offended. Here and there one, at least, would have been ready to say, with Wordsworth,—

"Me this unchartered freedom tires."

Little by little a reaction would have been produced, the "substratums and objects" of the land would have suffered disastrous eclipse, "feudal processes and poems" would have come in like a flood, and the last state of the national mind would have been worse than the first.

Nor can this extreme of revolt, or any approach to it, be thought necessary to constitute an American writer. "American" and "rebel" are not synonymous at this hour of the day. American literature, if we may assert our American right to speak a truism roundly, is literature written by Americans; that is to say, by the people of the United States. In its sub-

LACK OF AMERICAN LITERATURE 339

ject it may be old or new, domestic or foreign; it may be written in dialect, — sometimes called American, — or in English; in any case, if it is literature at all, it is American literature. And since there is already a body of such writing, we may venture upon another capital letter, by the compositor's leave, and speak of it — still modestly, and remembering its youth — as American Literature. For youthful it is, in the nature of the case, with its character but imperfectly formed, and its full share of juvenile foibles; still showing, as is inevitable and not discreditable, abundant traces of its English origin.

Thus far, it must be owned, it can boast little or no representation among the supremely great of the earth. The genius of a new country produces men of action rather than poets and philosophers. Washington and Lincoln are names to shine in any company, but as yet the roll of American authors contains few Homers and Shakespeares, and no great number of Dantes and Miltons. Such as they are, however, they are our own, and though in some cases we might have wished them more "distinctively American," we need not be in haste on that account to tag them with a foreign label. Neither need we delude ourselves with the notion that they might have been transcendent geniuses, all of them, had they but stood up resolutely against the English tradition. How to become a genius is one of the hard problems. There is no likelihood that it can be solved by any process of intellectual jingoism. The secret may consist partly in being one's self; pretty certainly it does not consist in being different from somebody else. Between imitation and a set attempt to avoid imitation there is not so very much to choose. Either of them stamps the work as secondary. As for Homers and Shakespeares, we may remember for our comfort that names like these are not to be found, in any country, among the living: they never have been.[1]

For our comfort, too, though not in the every-day sense of that word, we do well

[1] According to an eminent French critic, M. de Wyzewa, the United States still has (since Whitman's death, he means to say) two poets, — Mr. Merril and Mr. Griffin. "Only two" is the critic's phrase, but the adverb need not disturb us. A busy people who have two poets at once may count themselves rich.

to remind ourselves that as the greatness of our American authors is but relative, so is the newness of our American spirit. All that is called new is born of the old, and is itself in part old. The movement of history is not by successive creations of something out of nothing, but by the development of one thing from another; and whether we like to believe it or not, this that we call the American idea stands within the general law: it has been evolved, or rather it is being evolved, out of what was before it. The public mind, stirred by patriotic impulses and restive under criticism, may clamor for originality, meaning by that absolute novelty, and North, South, East, and West may exhaust themselves to answer the appeal: we shall never see an absolutely new book, be it the "great American novel" or anything else. As time goes on, we shall have, by the slow processes of nature, a literature more and more distinctive, more and more independent, and more and more unlike the English, more and more American; but to the end its originality, like that of all literature, will be but relative. Though men cross the sea, they can never escape the spirit of their forerunners. Our very rebelliousness against English domination is an English trait. The great American book, when it comes, will not spring from virgin soil, but from seed, and the seed will have had an age-long ancestry. "Works proceed from works," says a learned French critic; and the most searching of American critics had something of the same thought in mind when he wrote, fifty years ago, in response to inquiries "in Cambridge orations and elsewhere" for "that great absentee," an American literature, "A literature is no man's private concern, but a secular and generic result."

What then? Shall we cease effort, and leave it to blind law to work out for us our intellectual salvation? That would be childish. Because one thing is true, it does not follow that another and seemingly contradictory thing may not be true likewise. The same Emerson who spoke of literature as a "generic result," — a word so anticipatory of later thought as to seem like a flash of genius, — and therefore "no man's private concern," was never done with proclaiming the power of the individual soul and the omnipotence of individual faith. He never scolded his countrymen; he cherished no illusion about the ability of the American people or any other to hurry the accomplishment of a "secular result;" but he, more than all others combined, enforced the duty of American scholars to free themselves from the swaddling-clothes of tradition; to live in the present, think in the present, believe in the present, and speak always their own word. And the French critic just now quoted, so modern in his point of view, so very different in many respects from Emerson, — though Emerson, too, believed the laws and powers of the intellect to be "facts in a natural history," and so "objects of science," — was quoted but in part. "In literature as in art," he says, "the great operative cause — after the influence of individuality — is that of works upon works." The words are those of M. Brunetière, who, in his attempt to apply to literary criticism the methods of natural science, has seemed sometimes to allow more than enough to the power of things over thought; yet he, too, treating of the evolution of literary forms, gives the first place in that evolution, not to changed conditions, nor to the germinal force of great models, nor to the "moment," a word on which he greatly insists, but to the power of the individual.

And where ought this power of the individual to be quickly and strongly felt, if not in a democracy and in a new world?

Like many other good things, nevertheless, individuality, though it may properly be sought, is not to be gone after too directly, — as if it could be carried by assault. Originality has often suffered violence, it is true, but the violent have never taken it by force. We are not to hope for intellectual life by any process of spontaneous generation; nor are we to dread abjectly the influence of other minds over our own. Individuality is a gift rarely lost, except by those who lose it before they are born. Franklin, it is universally agreed, was an American of the most pronounced type, one of our greatest and most original men. His style, as Mr. James says of Lowell's, was "an indefeasible part of him;" yet all the world knows that he formed it, or believed that he formed it, by a studious imitation of Addison. Originality is theirs to whom it is given. With it a man may drench himself in the wisdom of the ages, and take no harm; without it he may eschew books never so jealously, and look into his own heart with never so complete a faith, and come to no good.

All of which is not to say that a scholar may not occupy himself too much with the thoughts of others to the neglect of his own, or that Americans as a people may not defer unreasonably to foreign standards. Between the two extremes, excessive dependence upon tradition and a too exclusive confidence in one's own genius, there is a middle course. If we cannot find it, then we are not yet ripe for a great national literature, which must be the result of the old culture bestowed upon new soil in a new time and under new conditions.

LIBRARY OF DAVIDSON COLLEGE

Books on regular loan may be checked out for **two weeks.** Books must be presented at the Circulation Desk in order to be renewed.

A fine of **five cents** a day is charged after date due.

Special books are subject to special regulations at the discretion of library staff.